STENDHAL
Fiction and the Themes of Freedom

STENDHAL

Fiction and the Themes of Freedom

VICTOR BROMBERT

The University of Chicago Press

Chicago and London

for Beth
for Gino Magnani
ricordando le ore emiliane . . .

. . . *every book ought to be read with the
same spirit and in the same manner as it is writ.*

—FIELDING

The University of Chicago Press, Chicago 60637
The University of Chicago Press, Ltd., London

Copyright ©1968 by the University of Chicago. All rights reserved
Published 1968. Midway Reprint 1976
Printed in the United States of America

International Standard Book Number: 0-226-07548-6
Library of Congress Catalog Card Number: 75-37057

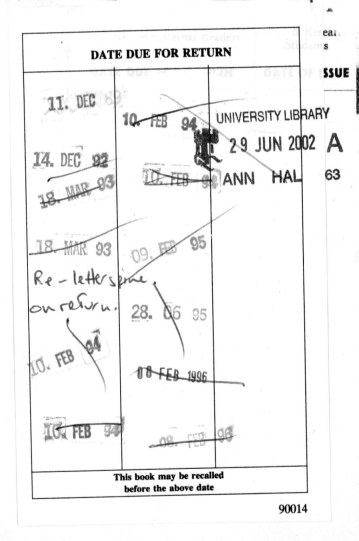

Foreword

Thematic criticism seems to me valuable when it is ultimately more concerned with the author's art and vision
than with any single motif or obsession. It has been my
attempt in this study to focus on the recurrence and variations of a central, unifying theme, without losing sight of
the issues raised by Stendhal's work and of the specific
quality of individual texts.

The themes of freedom invite an analysis of Stendhal's
novels on many levels of meaning. It is this multiplicity
of levels—this steady interweaving and counterpoint of
social, political, psychological, and ethical preoccupations
—that constitutes, in my opinion, the poetic density of
Stendhal's work. And beyond Stendhal, these themes of
freedom point to some of the central problems raised by
the nineteenth-century novel.

V. B.

Contents

1

the Temptations of Autobiography

THE VOICES OF THE SELF

Some fervent lovers of Stendhal would cheerfully relinquish one of his major novels in exchange for yet another volume of his unfinished autobiography, *Vie de Henry Brulard*. These fanatical "Brulardistes" make up the extreme wing of that self-recruiting sect of happy few known as Beylistes. Henri Beyle, their hero, is for them not merely the creator of Julien Sorel and Fabrice del Dongo, but a supreme master of the art of life, the very model of the free man, and a spiritual ally in their quest for sincerity. In him they irreverently revere the incarnation of paradoxes: the tender cynic, the passionate ironist, the self-conscious nonconformist, the lucid daydreamer.

For Beylisme is not so much a set of beliefs as a complex of attitudes. It suggests a special sensibility as well as a way of masking it, an unpretentious and unsentimental self-centeredness, a stance that is both pleasure-seeking and almost austere in its refinement.

It is Stendhal the novelist, rather than Beyle the egotist, who interests us: his themes, his techniques, his vision as transmuted and realized in the work of fiction. Yet *Henry Brulard* may well serve as a valuable starting point. True, Stendhal undertook this self-exploration in the autumnal years of his life, during his consular exile in Civitavecchia, when he discovered the fascination and consolatory thrills of long backward glances. But the resilient text of *Henry Brulard,* in which he relives with zestful precision the affective moods of his childhood, plunges us into the midst of typical Stendhalian problems. More explicitly than anywhere else, the author reveals his basic attitudes, his most intimate modes of feeling, as well as his permanent obsession with the riddle of the personality.

Fiction and biography are in fact intimately bound up in the Stendhalian context, not merely in the ordinary genetic sense, but in the very manner in which Stendhal understood the "metaphysics" of fiction. The writing of his novels corresponds to the quest for an elusive synthesis of being and existence. Biography and fiction dramatize with particular sharpness and complexity the irresolvable tension between man's concept of his destiny and of his freedom. For fiction, as well as biography, brings into permanent clash not only antagonistic temporal orders, but independent and frequently conflicting manifestations of human freedom: that of the "self," or objectified character as project and desiderative agent, and that of the author as observer-judge in search of meaning. This cleavage is, of course, an essential experience of the autobiographer. And these tensions, which characterize all fictional constructs as well, are at the heart of Stendhalian dialectics. They account in large part for the ambiguities of his tone and of his style.

The autobiographic urge became particularly acute after 1831, when the boredom of consular chores, as well as the self-imposed censorship of the newly appointed official of Louis-Philippe's government, apparently discouraged any sustained creative effort. In a letter to Henri Dupuy (23 June 1832), the author of the recently published *Le Rouge et le Noir* states his intention not to have anything of his appear in print while in the employ of the government. But the demon of literature was stronger. In his peculiar "franglais" he soon admits to himself that the true vocation of his soul still remains *"to make* chef-d'oeuvre." [1] In fact the autobiographic temptation was not at all a retreat from literature, but the natural blossoming of a lifelong tendency. The many posthumously published texts and marginal commentaries bear testimony to his assiduous self-observation and self-assessment. From the time of his arrival in Paris as a provincial adolescent, he indulged in endless note taking, diaries, "psychological" discussions and dialogues with himself, intimate accounts, plans for amorous action, analyses of his defects and qualities, and almost clinical "self-consultations." Even some of the notations he scribbled on his clothes (cuffs, belts, or suspenders)—betray a permanent tendency to view himself as both object and subject. This creative disseverance is at the center of his adolescent *Journal* (1801–1823) and culminates in his two autobiographic masterpieces, *Souvenirs d'égotisme* (1832) and *Vie de Henry Brulard* (1835).

On the surface, *Souvenirs d'égotisme* (the word "égotisme" points to self-knowledge as much as to self-concern) provides lively sketches, heightened by impertinent comments, irrelevant flashbacks, and peppery anecdotes, of Stendhal's life in Paris during the years 1821–1830: his stay at the Hôtel de Bruxelles, his nostalgia for Milan and for Métilde Dembowski who would not yield, evenings at the Tracy's where he met the aging General Lafayette, midnight punches in the apartment of the opera star Mme Pasta, a trip to England and touching adventures with prostitutes, his relations with Mérimée, his frequentation of the Liberal group meeting at Delécluze. But the real subject is not his life during these specific years; it is the very possibility of writing autobiography, of discussing oneself—in other words, the vexing problem of sincerity.

But is sincerity enough? The eye cannot see itself, as Stendhal sadly observes in an almost existentialist mood. "Quel homme suis-je?" ("What kind of man am I?") is the question that appears on the very first page of *Souvenirs d'égotisme*. But where and how is one to find the answer? The anguish of an impossible lucidity is enough to create insomnia. "I do not know myself; that is what sometimes, when I think of it at night, torments me." The trouble is that not even the "others" are of help in this puzzled search for the self. Even to the most basic questions—is he clever? is he good? is he courageous?—no answer is forthcoming from the outside. Trapped between the urge to reveal himself and the fear of being penetrated by another's consciousness, Stendhal can only further complicate his search for the elusive self. The mask he always wears to protect his inner being does not help him unveil it to himself. Ultimately, only the creative act—

whether that of the autobiographer or of the novelist—
will permit him to reconstruct, or rather to construct, the
truth of himself. That, in a sense, is the great intuition
Stendhal had early in his life, long before he himself
knew that he was to become a creator of fiction. It explains not only his self-directed adolescent dialogues, but
his chronic tendency to treat himself as a "character" and
his obsessive fondness for pseudonyms.

Many of Stendhal's self-revelations and much of the
impertinent charm of *Vie de Henry Brulard* can be
found in the earlier autobiographic attempt *Souvenirs
d'égotisme*. Although Stendhal may have trouble knowing who he is, he does know with sharp clarity what he
hates and what he loves. And he hates many things: vul-
garians, extreme heat, superficial French wit, boredom
(which he always considered an irredeemable sin), the
ugliness of Paris, where, like Rousseau (perhaps because
he had read him too much), he deplored the absence of
mountains. He is, in fact, proud of his "irritabilité ner-
veuse"; though robust and even paunchy, he delights in
his own "délicatesse de nerfs italienne." But the aversions
he so zestfully evokes also account for his fervor. Stendhal's capacity for enthusiasm thrives on indignation and
displeasure. *Souvenirs d'égotisme* thus concurrently provides an inventory of loves: the operas of Cimarosa and
Mozart; Italy, and in particular Milan, his adopted fatherland; the pleasures of a beautifully made dress, of day-
dreams, of anonymous perambulations in strange cities.
The catalog is unpredictable; what counts is not the im-
pressiveness of the object, but the quality of the reaction.
Shivering with pleasure at the unexpected sound of familiar names, dreaming of the magic powers Tasso attributed to Angelica's ring, delighting in the servitudes of his

heart, Stendhal thoroughly enjoys his own inability to sound pompous. Much like Count Mosca in *La Chartreuse de Parme*, he preserves, close to the age of fifty, a freshness of sensations and an emotive vulnerability heightened by irony and lucidity. Even the writer's vocation is presented with lack of solemnity by means of the metaphor of the silkworm, who, when tired of eating, climbs up to make its prison of silk.

But the lightness of touch must not deceive. There is also the recurrent temptation of suicide: upon his return to Paris, after 1821, he is in the habit of drawing pistols in the margins of his manuscripts. There is the bitter pain of awakening, on certain mornings, to rediscover afresh his loneliness and despair. Above all, there is that typically Stendhalian *pudeur* or restraint, that muteness of strong emotions, that latent fear of being exposed and of cheapening what he holds most dear. He will thus always "skip happiness" for fear of deflowering it.

We are touching here on the all-important theme of dissimulation and disguise. "I would wear a mask with pleasure, I would change my name with joy." The primary urge is that of remaining impenetrable to the glance of others, "n'être pas deviné." To hide his wounds as well as his enthusiasms, Stendhal learns to parade as a cynic and becomes, as he puts it, the buffoon of his own soul. But to hide means to play a role, to become another. "I am used to appearing as the contrary of what I am." The taste for incognito, the need for a mask, is thus closely related to the urge to impersonate. Wearing a mask becomes a trying out of roles in the service of self-discovery as well as of escape. But, paradoxically, escape and the act of intellectual disguise serve as the instruments of an oblique confession and ultimately of the creative act. The effort to hide and the wish to be other than oneself play, in his case, into the hands of the novelist: they bring about a state of permanent flirtation with other selves.

Vie de Henry Brulard, written several years after *Souvenirs d'égotisme,* provides even more penetrating insights into the relationships between self-search, self-concealment, and fiction. The very use of a pseudonym for the title of an autobiography (though the initials H. B. correspond to Stendhal's real name, Henri Beyle) indicates a subject-object relationship that clearly separates the author from his protagonist. On another level, the choice of a pseudonym could be interpreted as an act of protest, as an affirmation of rupture with parental and social origins. The rejection of the patronym, as Jean Starobinski brilliantly argues, is thus not merely a substitute for parricide, but a refusal of any form of predestination.[2] The recurrent myth of a special birth in Stendhal's novels corresponds to the yearning to grant himself his own destiny. The author—"ens causa sui"—strives to become his own creator. In fact, the combined themes of liberation and self-identification are at the heart of *Vie de Henry Brulard.* His entire childhood appears to him as a confinement from which it is his compelling vocation to escape. The father image thus becomes the very symbol of ensnaring pettiness and oppression. The search for freedom and identity ("Qu'ai-je été, que suis-je?") corresponds to a father-rejection, which in the novels assumes the form of a father-search; and the search for an identity for which there exists no a priori tag in turn predisposes him to treat himself as his own "creation." The human being evoked thus appears simultaneously as the child he was and continued to be into adulthood—a free agent capable of surprising the author-observer—and as the fixed eye that assesses this child. Fragmentation and continuity, innocence and experience, time lived and time retrieved are here locked in a contrapuntal relationship.

The setting and movement of the opening scene communicate a double voice and the telescoping of a double temporal perspective. The narrator, from the Janiculo, surveys the Roman landscape. As he distinguishes Frascati and Castel-Gandolfo and, much nearer him, the orange trees of a monastery, he muses on the fact that in three months he will be fifty years old. Historical time is brought into juxtaposition with personal time: all of Roman history in a panoramic display—the tomb of Cecilia Metella, Saint Paul, the pyramid of Cestius, the palace of Monte Cavallo, the Appian Way, the gardens of the Pincio—is set against the dates of his private history—1783, 1793, 1803 . . . the Napoleonic era, and now, here and already almost past, the evanescent moment on this sunny 16 October 1832. For there is yet another contrast within the contrasted historical and personal times: the past and the present. ("All of ancient and of modern Rome . . ."; the day of the Battle of Wagram and today.) And yet all these elements seem to move and glide into one another. In this remarkable introduction, private reminiscences and lyric meditation merge to bring about a peculiar poetic movement, self-conscious, unstable, and, as it were, under the very sign of relativity.

This is not to underestimate the sheer documentary value of *Vie de Henry Brulard*, which tells us most of what we know about Stendhal's childhood in his native Grenoble. The manner in which, as a boy, he reacted to his bourgeois background and to his family attached to the Ancien Régime explains a great deal of his ambiguous feelings toward Napoleon, the Restoration, the July Monarchy, and the growing democratization of attitudes and tastes. Aristocratic by inclination and Jacobinic by reaction, Stendhal is a man of two centuries, condemned to look both forward and backward with almost equal doses of curiosity and nostalgia.

Contrasts and antitheses account indeed for the most habitual patterns of his imagination. His childhood world is sharply divided: on one hand, the petty, contemptible creatures (prefiguring his villainous Valenod and Rassi); on the other, the free spirits, the elect, the happy few. This chronic need to compare and contrast—these dynamics of contempt that account for the vigor of his lyric enthusiasms—finds an early expression in the manner in which he clearly separates the members of his own family into two irreconcilable camps. On his father's side is moroseness, bigotry, and uninspired materialism. Stendhal's father is for him the very embodiment of bourgeois provincialism, while the image of his mother, who died when he was only seven years old and for whom he claims to have felt the first transports of physical love ("I wanted to cover my mother with kisses, and also that she should have no clothes on"), symbolizes grace and poetic sensitivity. To this Gagnon side of his family he attributes an "Italian" origin, his own love for Tasso and Ariosto, and the uncalculating surrender to the passionate and generous movements of the soul, which he defines by the vaguely Corneillian concept of "Espagnolisme" of which his aunt Elizabeth is the outstanding incarnation. Espagnolisme and provincialism were of course destined to clash in his novels.

Stendhal does not claim that all his *facts* are correct; he never bragged about the accuracy of his memory. It is the emotional memory that he asks us to trust, echoing Rousseau, whose writings, especially the *Confessions* and *La Nouvelle Héloïse,* had a far greater influence on him than is commonly granted. Significantly, he refers to his autobiography as his own *Confessions,* "au style près, comme Jean-Jacques Rousseau . . ." [3] He is at his best when he recalls with amusing but painful vividness the humiliations, repressed hatreds, and suffered or imagined injustices. On his tyrannical aunt Séraphie, who took over the direction of the household after his mother's death; on the loathsome memories of Grenoble; on the hypocrisy of his Jesuit tutor, the abbé Raillane, who succeeded in making him hate religion forever, he rises to the height of indignation. There are the grim memories of an embittered and rebellious boy: his joy at the news of the king's execution, his thanking God at the time of his hated aunt's death. But there are also humorously tender and lyric moods: his discovery of *Don Quixote,* his decision to become another Molière, his enthusiasm for Bonaparte's dragoons passing through Grenoble on their way to Italy, his silent love for the actress Kubly, his clumsy behavior upon his arrival in Paris, and his ecstatic joy at crossing the Saint Bernard Pass and discovering Milan.

The problem of memory is at the center of the autobiographic enterprise. In the case of Stendhal, it casts a most revealing light on his creative processes. The inadequacies of memory invite not only discovery but also the compensatory assistance of imagination and interpretation. About Stendhal's own lack of faith in his recall and objectivity of information there can be no doubt. He knew that the 1835 perspective was different from that of 1790; he also knew that it was not possible to limit one's vision to a single temporal point of view. Moreover, the most blanked-out moments, the ones most difficult to resurrect in their entirety, are those of the most intense emotions—precisely the ones that count the most. These *"manques"* he compares to the ruined parts of a fresco. Yet, in the unevenness of remembrance, in the juxtaposition of luminously clear sectors of the past and of zones of meaningful emptiness, lurks the potential of the creative impulse. The multivalence of perspectives can be a source of error but also of invention. And the metaphor of the fresco suggests that entire areas could be restored. Repeatedly, Stendhal explains that he makes discoveries while writing: long-forgotten parts of the fresco "appear suddenly." Many things "come back in the process of writing." The re-creative act of evoking and explaining the past turns out to be primarily creative. Stendhal himself is the first to be surprised: seeking himself as he was in the past, he discovers himself as he is in the present, spontaneously reacting to his search.

Yet this "creative" discovery, or reinvention, implies not merely the blanking out of strong emotions within the author's memory but the elaborate camouflage of his most passionate commitments in his relations with others, and most specifically in his relations with his imagined reader. *Vie de Henry Brulard* admirably illustrates these forms of disguise, the fear of self-revelation that steadily accompanies the need to reveal himself. Thirst for candor goes hand in hand with joy of dissimulation. The young boy quickly learns that it is dangerous to convey one's enthusiasm to others and that, in the face of ironic smiles or reprobation, silence is the best protection: "During my entire life, I have never spoken about the object of my passion; the least objection would have pierced my heart." Revealing one's secret dreams may be the greatest wish; but it seems like blasphemy to the young Henri Beyle. Next to silence, the best protection of the secrets of one's inner life is the lie. "Mentir n'est-il pas la seule ressource des esclaves?"

The same tendencies appear in Stendhal's attitude toward the half-written page and, beyond the act of writing, in his relations with his unkown reader. "One spoils such tender feelings by describing them in detail." It is on this note of lyrical refusal that the text of *Vie de Henry Brulard* comes to an end. Happiness, in particular, whether upon his arrival in Milan or during his boyhood excursions to regions made famous by Rousseau, refuses to be encompassed and analyzed. Stendhal prefers the *negative* approach: to evoke the unpleasant condition from which this specific happiness is excluded. "The only way, it seems to me, in which I could paint a picture of this enchanting pleasure, pure, fresh, and divine, would be by enumerating the miseries and boredom by whose complete absence it was produced." Or, better still, there is the poetry of silence, that which Stendhal himself calls "le silence du bonheur"—the poetry of the unspoken, perhaps even of the unfulfilled. But such poetry, rooted in self-revelation and self-dissimulation, marks an essentially creative act. Fiction is here wedded to the dialectics of sincerity and alibis.

AUTOBIOGRAPHY AS FICTION

Sartre is no doubt right, at least in philosophical terms, in saying that one must choose between living one's life and viewing it from the outside like a work of art. To treat oneself, while alive, in a posthumous manner, to impose on one's existence a definitive or even temporary horizon, signifies a denial of life. One must be either inside or outside—one cannot be both.[4] For time itself is not reversible; and every act—including the act of writing autobiography—separates us from our past and modifies it. The principle of heterogeneity reigns between the past and the present. Man, by projecting his freedom into the act of living, affirms himself precisely as being *other* than his past.

In fact, any account of "meaningful" behavior, any value imposed by man on his own acts, derives from the imaginative process. Conversely, the creative enterprise implies a multiple perspective on the self. Thus all fiction tends to decipher a psychology in movement, while embodying at the same time the specific notion of "freedom" it seeks to communicate.

The paradox of the act of creation stands at the center of *Vie de Henry Brulard*. Stendhal was, moreover, perfectly lucid about it. He knew that he had undertaken not a simple recounting but an act of creation and that what he was creating was precisely the boy Henry Brulard, if not Beyle-Stendhal himself. The fictional tendency is quite explicit. Stendhal at one point asks his reader—taking for granted that Henry Brulard is really the name of the narrator (which is of course a prime element of fiction)—to imagine that the name Brulard had been replaced by Bernard: the result, he explains, would be "a novel written in the first person singular." The comment is made as a form of apology to justify the self-centered nature of the book. But the suggestion carries other implications as well: first of all that the appearance of subjectivity and objectivity can be misleading. Thus modern novelists have discovered that first-person narration allows for degrees of objectivity that the so-called omniscient and "objective" narration, because of the very involvement of an omnipresent author, cannot truly achieve. This paradox explains why Stendhal, at the very moment that he toys with the notion of a novelistic perspective (one of the first versions contains the significant *lapsus* "ce roman"), repeatedly utilizes the word "roman" in a derogatory sense. "Je ferais du roman," he warns himself, as he feels he is about to indulge in sheer invention. Fiction and untruth become almost synonymous. One is reminded of the fictional subversion of fiction as practiced by Diderot in *Jacques le Fataliste*. The self-mockery of the novelist's stance is not only a form of intellectual debunking but an oblique manner of affirming the independence of both narrator and character. The game, in either case, is in the service of freedom. But Stendhal's game is further complicated by the fact that his anti-novel is ostensibly not a novel at all.

"I am another man," writes Stendhal, as he compares the Henri Beyle of 1835 with the one of 1800. But this otherness is not exclusively temporal. "It seems to me that I am making discoveries about someone else." In a marginal commentary, Stendhal states his own surprise. Expressions such as "un autre" or "ce caractère" testify to a creative separation from himself. He indeed sees himself not merely as *having* but also as *being* a character. This *dédoublement* accounts in large part for his treatment of himself in the third person singular. "Henri B., age less than six years," he writes under one of the numerous little sketches that are props to his memory. Elsewhere he marvels at this "caractère de Henri." He objectifies himself in order to judge himself; but the reverse is also true: his commentaries, much like the novelist's intrusions in *Le Rouge et le Noir* or in *La Chartreuse de Parme,* protect the independence of his hero.

The explicit sense of treating himself as a protagonist is allied to the self-conscious awareness of having a prospective reader. Stendhal, seeker of sincerity, claims to write without lies and without illusions, as though he were addressing a letter to an intimate friend. But he is also writing for that distant and hypothetical creature he calls "mon lecteur" whose imagined reactions necessarily imply a literary strategy. Thus, in marginal comments, he shows his concern for dramatic development and for suspense: "Style. Ordre des idées. Préparer l'attention . . ." The speed with which he writes does not prevent him from worrying about sustaining the interest of his invisible reader. The presentation and construction of episodes trouble him. He wonders, for instance, whether or not the end of the chapter provides an apt conclusion to the episode of his childish infatuation with the actress Kubly. Elsewhere he expresses his dissatisfaction with the "scholarly coda" of a given paragraph. Hesitations such as these are reflected in the very body of the text. He promises himself that he will correct, transpose, eliminate certain passages. He refers to his life story as his "conte"; he is aware of composing a literary account. At one point, he even advises himself, in a parenthesis in English, to "cut there." This artistic self-consciousness is perhaps brought out most sharply in a musical metaphor (". . . il faudra que je travaille et transcrive ces morceaux") and in the humorous allusion to *Tristram Shandy* (". . . I am about to be born").

The awareness of the intangible but wished-for reader is the corollary of the author-protagonist relationship. The past self thus undergoes a steady process of heroization. Gilbert Durand very astutely points to the mythical dimension of *Vie de Henry Brulard*. The trivial detail is in fact never meant to be trivial; it appears wearing the buskin, and suggests the forces of a destiny.[5] The almost archetypal patterns of Stendhal's autobiography deserve to be studied in greater detail; they cast light not merely on this specific text, but on the structure, deeper motifs, and texture of his novels.

The most significant among these patterns is conveyed through the family myth. Henry Brulard's hatred of his father is not a fortuitous factor to be dismissed as a regrettable antipathy and the original cause of the young boy's rebellious nature. Its deeper significance is that it justifies and almost requires the notion of a double paternity. Stendhal repeatedly explains that his "true father" was his grandfather, Dr. Gagnon. It was he, much like the surgeon-major in *Le Rouge et le Noir* and the abbé Blanès in *La Chartreuse de Parme*, who initiated the young boy to the spiritual life. In fact, Dr. Gagnon's lessons in astronomy, during the summer nights on top of the mysterious terrace of his house, seem endowed with a magic quality and prefigure the astrological apprenticeship of Fabrice in the priest's tower. Such an initiatory prestige explains why his grandfather's lineage seems to him "dear and sacred." Inadvertently—the *lapsus* is revealing—he refers to himself as the "fils de M. Gagnon," thus substituting for the reality of his father's paternity the fiction of a maternal begetting, a fiction in which he indulges all the more freely because his mother died when he was a small boy.

The father-rejection is deeply involved with an identity-creating search for the true father. Stendhal's family myth, a recurrent motif in his novels, is further nourished by repeated suggestions of "exceptional" origins and of an almost miraculous birth and development. The young boy's dreams of freedom go hand in hand with dreams of prestigious ancestors. "Might I not be the son of a great prince . . . ?" he asks himself half seriously, as he constructs what he calls the "fable" of his formative years. This "fabulous" background and education are corroborated, in his view, by the melodramatic escape to Avignon of his mother's putative Italian ancestor after he committed a crime of passion. The myth of Italy, so important in Stendhal's work, is thus linked with the combined themes of energy and of an ineffable beauty.

This toying with fictional and mythical possibilities is stressed by a steady, though ironic, dramatization of his childhood. He insists on his difference from other children, on his enforced segregation (his family did not allow him to play in the street), on his withdrawal and capacity to "dream alone." Like Rousseau, whose *Confessions* were obviously on his mind while writing *Vie de Henry Brulard,* he discovers, as a mere child, the brutal reality of the world's injustice and of his vocation as a rebel. The sufferings of young Henry are presented as elements of a broader dramatic development. He literally refers to the "sad drama of my childhood" and to the "personages" with whom, or rather against whom, this drama is played out. But this suffering itself is not an ordinary, fruitless suffering; it is the indispensable and self-redeeming apprenticeship of the hero. Just as all the "malheur" of his life in Grenoble made possible the "bonheur" of his life in Milan (the principle of value-by-contrast is once more verified), so the very tyranny of his education played into the hands of liberty. Stendhal significantly speaks of a "happy unhappiness" (an "heureux malheur"). Even the boy's first amorous experience, combining anguish and frustration, brings about a tragic illumination. Love, he discovered, is "a serious and fearful thing."

The sense of loss and nostalgia, singularly unsentimental, likewise points to a myth-making tendency. Henry's childhood, viewed as a private golden age, is thus linked with the prestige of a bygone period (the elegance of the Ancien Régime) or with the dynamic virtues of the Revolutionary and Bonapartist epoch. Stendhal repeatedly establishes temporal and affective parallels between his personal existence and the drama of modern history. This insertion into a historic continuum extends to literary history as well. His satisfaction at having witnessed, as a young boy, the end of Mme de Merteuil's world is not simply a reference to Laclos' *Les Liaisons dangereuses,* but confers a retrospective aura on the otherwise lusterless daily existence of a clumsy provincial boy. This ironically poetic illumination and amplification of the trivial events of an existence—an illumination that transforms this existence into a destiny—finds its most symbolic expression in the transmutation of the countryside near the family property in Echelles into the scene of Tasso's *Gerusalemme liberata.*

Metaphoric visions of the décor go with metaphoric visions of the self. Stendhal recalls himself as a little Tasso at the age of sixteen: "un centième du Tasse," he adds modestly. There is irony in the parallel. But there is also a characteristic esthetic elaboration of the raw materials of his existence. He casts himself not only into the roles of significant artists (he almost becomes a reincarnation of Rousseau as he arrives in the land of Zulietta), but far more revealingly into existing roles: as an amorous character in Voltaire's *Zadig* writing the initials of his beloved in the sand, as Laurence Sterne's protagonist, as Beaumarchais' Chérubin timidly in love with love, as a paradoxical mixture of Saint-Preux and Valmont. And in the midst of his own esthetic construction, he sees himself surrounded by "personages" straight out of a bitter comedy by Molière. This metaphoric vision, a transfiguration of self, finds its most acute and its most humorous expression in repeated artistic and historical analogues, which transform young Henry now into a painted figure of a compassionate Saint John, now into a typical Roman Stoic, now again into a rebellious people ineffectively tyrannized by myopic popes, medieval potentates, or contemporary despots. "All tyrannies resemble each other." This remark also serves to remind us that, in the case of Stendhal, the sense of personal drama is inextricably linked to a passionate concern with the drama of history.

The fictional virtualities of *Vie de Henry Brulard* are further brought out by elements of literary construction, dual perspectives, and speculative rumination. The apparently capricious, ambling, and digressive development obeys in part certain inner laws that are more significant than the laws of chronology. Stendhal exploits titillating delays, accelerations, and shortcuts. His elliptic résumés and prolepses, his techniques of approximations and amplifications, all serve to direct the reader's reactions and to shape apparently casual accounts into patterns of mean-

ing. The playful creation of hypothetical situations and
the ironic toying with other possibilities for a given scene
or a given action are indirect ways of imposing, or super-
imposing, fictional structures. In his novels also, Stendhal
shows himself fond of the conditional approach, which
serves to introduce at almost every point new levels of fiction. Henry Brulard is thus seen as a would-be rascal, a
"coquin," who might have immorally acquired an immense
fortune, or as a lackey in the service of a Neapolitan
composer. Stendhal goes so far as to provide hypothetical
dialogues. Even his self-directed irony assumes a hypothetical quality, as he imagines, for instance, the verbal-
ized opinions of Count Daru discovering that his much-
recommended protégé—this "brilliant humanist"—cannot
even spell an ordinary word correctly.

Stendhal delights in distorting, correcting, or compensating what was with what might have been. Thus two
separate voices are almost constantly at play—voices that
correspond to the two temporal orders: time in its fragmentary and spontaneous immediacy as it is apprehended
moment by moment, and time as a continuous and meaningful flow when it is viewed in retrospect. But sophisticated retrospection in turn brings about a nostalgia for
the poetic voice of inexperience. Stendhal is, of course, perfectly aware of the interlocked double points of view.
After attributing a shrewd piece of strategy to the boy
Henry, he adds: "But I find this reasoning a bit ahead of
his age." Nonetheless, he takes pleasure in juxtaposing,
combining, and confusing the two perspectives. At times,
the very same sentence carries a dual effect. "For more
than a month I was proud of this vengeance; this trait
pleases me in a child." At other times, it is not a blending
but a contrast that is effected: Ariosto as seen by the infat-

uated young reader and Ariosto as judged by the sophisticated (and opinionated) man of letters are far from one
and the same thing. Stendhal finds a scandalized enjoy-
ment in this strabismus, or obliquity of vision. "But, good
heavens! who will read this? what gibberish! . . . Does
the reader know now whether he is in 1800, with a mad-
man's start in life, or with the wise reflection of a man
of fifty-three?"

The counterpoint of the two voices serves both a
thematic and a dramatic function. Much as in Proust's
novel, where the narrator's voice of analysis and worldliness constantly clashes with the voice of poetic immediacy, so in *Vie de Henry Brulard,* though in a different
register, a retrospective sense of necessity constantly plays
against and paradoxically underscores the motifs of spontaneity and freedom. For the retrospective orientation, as
Gilbert Durand points out, is frequently of an "oracular"
nature.[6] It would be easy to illustrate Stendhal's repeated
suggestion that all that happened pointed forward, that
his past is a permanent projection into the future, that all
his childhood experiences are properly part of a meaningful apprenticeship. Whether it be his vocation as unhappy
lover or his first descent into suffering, his past is filled
with significant thresholds and omens. His mother's death
is not an end but a beginning: "là véritablement a com-
mencé ma vie morale . . ."

Even more obvious are the proleptic techniques by
means of which the author repeatedly reminds his reader
that this is not a mere string of anecdotes and discon-
nected reminiscences, but that he has a "story" to tell.
"Soon after, the famous letter arrived . . ." Similarly,
Stendhal announces that he will soon speak of the military campaigns of 1800, of 1809, of the retreat from

Moscow, of the campaign of 1813. Whether or not he fulfills these promises is another matter. What counts is the feeling of impending events. This suspense technique is humorously summed up in Chapter 33, when Henry Brulard is compared to a great but still tranquil river about to be precipitated into an immense cascade.

What emerges, despite Stendhal's love of masks and disguises, is a solidarity with what he takes to be his destiny, which also assumes a negative quality: he may not know what he is, but he does know what he would not have wanted to be. Certainly he would have wanted to be neither Félix Faure nor Edouard Mounier, his old friends who are now *pairs de France*. Whatever the riddle of his own personality, he prefers himself to others. Thus the events of his life all contribute toward a singular elaboration of the self. Nothing is really a chance occurrence—or rather, even chance is made to contribute toward a goal. "Chance has guided me by the hand in five or six important circumstances in my life. I truly owe *Fortune* a little statue." Even incidental, self-mocking commentaries reveal the same fatidic pattern. "God destined me to have good taste," writes Stendhal the atheist, remembering how as a boy he felt critical of vulgar erotic engravings in Voltaire's *La Pucelle*.

How is one to reconcile this satisfied acceptance of circumstances with the tensions of a will bent on affirming itself in the very process of living? To be sure, Stendhal insists on the young boy's resolution: "At the age of seven, I had resolved to write comedies like Molière." Or again: "From that point on my vocation had been decided: to live in Paris, while writing comedies like Molière." But such assertions, within the structure and texture of the book, hardly dismiss the paradox that poses destiny against a quest for freedom. This fundamental paradox is further heightened by Stendhal's cult of the *imprévu,* by his cult of energy. Only a binocular exposure, implying an orientation and a perspective strictly opposed to the oracular viewpoint, can protect spontaneity and freedom. Thus Stendhal exploits, simultaneously with omniscient effects, the liberating resources of a limited horizon.

Georges Blin has masterfully analyzed the techniques of the "restriction de champ" as they appear in the novels.[7] This subjective restriction of the field of vision, implying a glance that is free from the tyranny of foresight and ubiquity, manifests itself repeatedly, in *Vie de Henry Brulard,* through a fade-in technique that leads us, by way of the protagonist's consciousness, directly into a given situation. Awareness is always fragmentary. "Without knowing how I arrived there, I see myself in the little room Gros occupied . . ." These repeated autobiographic *medias res* ("je me vois marchant . . ."; "je me vois logé . . ."; "Tout à coup je me vois . . .") provide a sense of contingency and unpredictability.

All fiction no doubt depends on this subtle interplay of necessity and gratuity. The balance and dosage may vary; the synthesis of being and existing may be more or less satisfactorily achieved. But this fundamental tension is what makes *Vie de Henry Brulard* an enterprise of the imagination as much as of memory, what makes it in fact a work of creative retrospection. Nothing is more revealing in this respect than Stendhal's habit of toying with the other possibilities of an irreversible occurrence. This conditional, speculative approach to the past, which makes him wonder whether any of his interpretations is valid, typically introduces a transfiguring element into many of his reminiscences. "I ruminate incessantly on what interests me; by considering it from different *positions of the soul,* I end up by seeing something new, and I make it *change its aspect.*" This crucial statement in Chapter 31 clearly indicates not only how the ability to relive with intensity is related to the very intensity of "doubt," but also, conversely, how this speculative approach, which accompanies the intensity of memory, stirs the powers of the imagination.

If the mystery of the personality explains Stendhal's self-search and self-creation, his literary enterprise, in turn, exploits this mystery as its central subject. More often than in *Souvenirs d'égotisme,* Stendhal, in his account of his childhood in *Vie de Henry Brulard,* insists on this elusiveness of the character, on its mobile and protean nature. "I will be fifty years old; it would be high time to know myself. What have I been, what am I?" But in fact, he does not know and cannot answer. He repeatedly eludes himself. The mobility of the observer makes it doubly difficult to fix the mobility of the subject. Thus Stendhal, by the very nature of his own awareness of the self, is led to develop the themes of motion, restlessness, instability, change, and continuous becoming. These will be the themes of his novels as well as the principles of their built-in subversion, because the impossibility of confining and defining reality, of making literature and life coincide, is at the heart of Stendhal's literary venture. An instrument of self-criticism, his writing is for him also an instrument of discovery, in the process of which memory and imagination become interchangeable, and cerebral masquerades serve his pursuit of truth.

2

ARMANCE

the
Apprenticeship
of Fiction

FALSE PATHS

This chapter might well be skipped by readers impatient to reach Stendhal's masterpieces, *Le Rouge et le Noir* and *La Chartreuse de Parme*. But the hard fact of the matter is that Stendhal wrote his first novel—not a superior one at that—at the age of forty-four. He had already published half a dozen books, and nothing, at least on the surface, seemed to indicate that the dilettantish lover of art and music, the pungent polemicist and ironic traveler, would try his hand at fiction. Nothing in fact would have surprised the plagiarist-author of *Histoire de la peinture en Italie* or the political satirist of *Rome, Naples et Florence* more than the prophecy that he was destined to become one of the most original novelists of France. This delay and this apparent unpredictability are in themselves worthy of some comment.

In the years following his return from Italy—he was then reaching his forties—Stendhal was known in Parisian circles as a witty and sarcastic conversationalist. Those familiar with his writings might have appreciated his highly irreverent attacks against the Winckelmannian concept of ideal beauty, his fresh though amateurish views on opera buffa, his ironic brand of liberalism, his sarcastic vein. When *Racine et Shakespeare* appeared in two parts (1823, 1825), it became clear that his was one of the significant militant voices on the side of Romanticism, although his particular approach to the literary debate was colored by the politically oriented "Romanticist" group of Milan. His allies admired his caustic pen. Those whom he irritated saw in him either a subversive Jacobin or a buffoonish cynic. But neither friend nor foe could have detected the least evidence that this apparently incorrigible amateur had the gifts and the vision of a truly creative artist.

To be sure, Henri Beyle himself, ever since his early days in Grenoble, dreamed of literary fame. But he sought to achieve this fame as a dramatist. His aim, even as a child, was to be a new Molière. To write "serious" comedies had been his most lasting ambition. His chief occupation as an adolescent in Paris was not the pursuit of mathematics, as he promised his father, but assiduous attendance at the theater. He watched and recorded with equal concentration the unfolding of the play, the performances of the artists, and the reaction of the public—in the hope that somehow these would deliver to him the secret of success. He even enrolled as a student in the speech and acting classes of the famous Dugazon, partly to lose his Dauphinois accent, partly in the hope of meeting some not too recalcitrant young actress, but largely to study at close range the practical problems of dramaturgy.

Although Molière, Shakespeare, and Alfieri were his idols, Stendhal's own attempts at playwriting were to remain abortive. Later, administrative duties, the war, self-imposed exile, and financial difficulties damped his ardor, but the dream of theatrical glory was indeed slow to die. All that now remains of endless projects, outlines, and drafts is a number of mediocre verses, in addition to clear proof of Stendhal's satiric intentions and of his fascination with subjects of contemporary relevance.

This raises questions that reach beyond the specific case of Stendhal. Why is it that his first ambition was not to write successful novels? Certainly he knew and loved *La Nouvelle Héloïse* and *Les Liaisons dangereuses*. They had been early models; in his mind Saint-Preux and Valmont continued to act out a crucial dialectic conflict. He appreciated the finesse and insights of *La Princesse de Clèves*, the brio of Diderot's *Jacques le Fataliste* and of Fielding's "immortal" *Tom Jones*. Why then did he not try to follow in these footsteps? The answer applies to Stendhal as well as to young Balzac and countless other seekers of literary fame at the beginning of the nineteenth century: the novel was simply not a road to quick or sensational success. The lure of the theater, with its promise of immediate glory, audible applause, money, and women, was far greater.

Conversely, and despite the great novelists of the previous century, the novel around 1820 did not enjoy any real prestige. Boileau, the literary legislator of French Classicism, had refused to consider it an honorable genre. This canon was still accepted; the novel was considered a minor, generally frivolous form of literary entertainment whose subject, usually an insipid variation of the love motif, rarely dealt with serious issues. We are still far from the summas of Balzac, Dostoyevsky, or Proust. Nobody in 1820 could have predicted that the novel was soon to usurp the traditional preeminence of dramatic and epic poetry. Stendhal's own opinion of the novel remained characteristically unexalted even after he finished *Le Rouge et le Noir*. In an outline of a review of his own novel sent to an Italian friend, he maintains that the "enormous consumption" of works of fiction is primarily a feminine phenomenon, that the devouring of novels is the chief occupation of provincial women, and that the subjects and perspective are consequently designed for a low reading level. True enough, he prides himself on having created a hero who is not always absurdly "perfect" and who is placed in a context of social and psychological realism. But the very fact that he insists on the exceptional and even daring aspects of his book implicitly suggests a condemnation of the general output of fictional literature.

A further question must be raised: given the prestige of the theater and the lusterless status of the novel, why did Stendhal, like innumerable gifted writers, fail as a playwright, fail even to pursue this seemingly attractive road for very long? Balzac, and later Flaubert, Baudelaire, and Zola, all faced disappointing experiences. Could it be, in all these cases, a simple lack of talent? Certainly Stendhal confronted some almost insurmountable handicaps: totally ungifted as a versifier, his approach to dramaturgy was overly schematic and his verbal inventiveness barely adequate. In fairness, however, other reasons must be furnished. New social conditions, in the wake of the Revolution, had brought about commercialization of the theater and had given rise to a heterogeneous public, which made it increasingly difficult for an author to establish a nuanced rapport with his audience. Censorship, always more vigilant in the performing arts, had reduced the theater to intellectual aridity during the Napoleonic régime. Matters did not improve under the Restoration. Figaro's complaint that every subject worth talking about was taboo proved to be truer in 1810 and 1815 than in the days of Beaumarchais.

Stendhal became keenly aware of these difficulties. In a text significantly entitled *La Comédie est impossible en 1836*, he shows how a young author, despairing of a mixed and largely unpolished public incapable of appreciating either his tone or his insights, is bound to fall back on the *comédie-roman* and ultimately on the novel, which at least offers the advantage of addressing itself to one reader at a time. A marginal comment in a copy of *Le Rouge et le Noir* is even more explicit: "Impossibility of Comedy since the Revolution; two audiences, the vulgar and the refined . . ." [1] Significantly, this "impossibility" of comedy is related, in Stendhal's mind, to the emergence of the novel as the only literary form in which some measure of "truth" can be achieved. He recalls M. de Tracy's opinion: "on ne peut plus atteindre au vrai que dans le Roman." And in a letter to Vincenzo Salvagnoli (2 November 1832), he notes that the taste for novels is gradually replacing, in France as well as in England, the fondness for plays. The reason, he feels, is that the playwright is forced into rehashing the same worn-out subjects, whereas fiction promises many as yet uncharted zones. Above all, things detailed and complex in manner can be said in the novel that could not possibly be presented on the stage. *Maxima debetur puero reverentia.* In the theater, certain proprieties and a certain decorum must be respected. "Everything, on the contrary, can be said in a novel." Stendhal, prophetically, announces what he calls the *Roman nouveau.*

AN APPRENTICESHIP

Yet, considered retrospectively, his abortive efforts at playwriting were not wasted. He learned the art of dramatic exposition, of preparations, of setting up scenes, of dramatic contrasts. He practiced his comic inventiveness, and some of the most successful "scenes" in his novels— Madame de Rênal's handling of her jealous husband, the Prince-Sanseverina-Mosca trio in *La Chartreuse*—retain an undeniable theatrical flavor. Most important, however, Stendhal learned to meditate on the author's relationship to his public and on the strategy of literary expression. The simultaneous pursuit of dramaturgical dreams and of an "ideological" education is not fortuitous. For Ideology —the antimetaphysical, sensualist, and utilitarian system of the school of Condillac—fed not only his rationalism and anticlericalism but his need to classify, analyze, and understand psychological motives and character development as well. Self-revelation was, so he felt, the best instrument for self-control, just as the understanding of others was the indispensable condition for skillful manipulation of their emotions.

During his early years in Paris, Stendhal assiduously pursued an education in Ideology, with Helvétius, Lancelin, and Destutt de Tracy as his intellectual idols. But just as one should not exaggerate the importance of this adolescent fervor, so it would be wrong to deny the value of this apprenticeship. The lesson of these masters was useful in purging him of too concentrated a dose of Rousseauistic sentimentality, even though its actual substance was metamorphosed and assimilated into Beylisme in the most unpredictable manner. From the Idéologues, Stendhal learned that analysis could be an instrument of the will, that to make others will against their instinct or disposition was a supreme intellectual achievement. The philosophical example of Lancelin here merged with the literary lesson of Valmont and of the Marquise de Merteuil. But he also learned that character is determined and revealed by man's particular way of seeking happiness, in other words, that *passion* is not a destructive and reprehensible force, but the mainspring of energy, and as such to be cultivated for its own sake. Finally, he derived from his philosophical readings a master lesson in emancipation and freedom to which, in touchingly proselytizing fashion, he tried to convert his more convention-bound sister, Pauline. The letters to Pauline, in which he poses as a self-styled teacher and initiator, read in fact like an elementary course in Ideology. Yet, two themes, which turn out to be crucial in Stendhal's vision as man and novelist, emerge from these naïve résumés and definitions: faith in the freedom-giving power of analysis and knowledge (the emancipation of women thus appears primarily as an educational problem), and the need to resist the tyrannical pressures of society by avoiding a direct clash and by adopting, if need be, the very techniques of a much hated hypocrisy. Ideology thus turns out to be a double lesson in self-assertion and in self-protection, deeply related to the major Stendhalian themes of freedom.

In the juvenile notes gathered under the title *Pensées. Filosofia Nova*,[2] Stendhal applies the analytical method of his beloved Ideology to his literary projects. From 1802 to 1805, the would-be creator of comedies dutifully analyzes the secrets of dramaturgical formulas and indulges in general considerations on the artist's intellectual hygiene. An excess of classifications and self-administered advice may have had something to do with the author's artistic paralysis. But the discipline of literary self-analysis and self-awareness, incompatible as it is with the myth of Stendhal the improvisor, was to have lasting results. For Stendhal's art is the product not only of a long rehearsal but also of an extreme sensitivity to the reactions of an imagined reader. This self-conscious awareness of the reader, which later manifests itself through the pirouettes of a self-protective irony, shows up, in *Pensées. Filosofia Nova*, through concerns of a strictly tactical nature. Thus Stendhal believes that in order to succeed one must first know, then flatter the audience. "Before writing comedies and tragedies it is necessary to determine what spectators one wants to please." This remark is to be supplemented by the following: "To succeed, I must flatter my contemporaries . . ." We are far indeed from the image of Stendhal as the nonconformist challenger of established values, yet not quite so far as might seem, if one remembers that Ideology taught Stendhal that the understanding of others was the preliminary step in the long-range strategy of controlling their desires and tastes.

Equally interesting are the technical and stylistic problems that are raised. Under the influence of Alfieri, Stendhal toys with the idea of subjects focused exclusively on a single protagonist. This limitation and concentration worries the putative playwright, but prefigures the novelist's technique of reducing his vision to the subjectivity of a central character. Stendhal also conceives of a hero who would be heroic to the extent that he is unaware of it ("the true hero accomplishes his beautiful deed without suspecting that it is beautiful"); but such undramatic innocence implies a telescoping of the character's and of the author's perspective, and an ambivalence that fiction can provide more readily than drama. At every point, though apparently concerned with the problem of writing for the stage, Stendhal raises questions that, if carried to their logical extreme, would lead him to the novel. His remarks on the "vibrato" of style, on the relation between rhythm and the "liaison of ideas," on the "charming familiarity" of Montaigne's tone, or on the all-importance of the "unexpected" (*"le soudain"*) have more to do with the processes of narration than with character revelation in a dramatic context. Revealingly, though it is not related to his immediate concerns, he devotes an entire page to Fielding's *Tom Jones*. Revealingly also, though in a negative manner, he defines those areas that, according to him, are best suited to fiction. In one of the most interesting entries, he notes that "bourgeois tragedy" is not the proper subject for the theater but for the novel. Elsewhere, he observes that hidden passions, particularly those that the characters try to hide from themselves, cannot be adequately presented on the stage. He is thus led to imagine a realistic, minute-by-minute account, a stenographic "procès-verbal," not of the outward deeds of a given character, but of the "operations of his head and of his soul." The possibility of an accurate stenography of the spirit fascinates the young Stendhal. (II, 179–180)

While flirting with theories and alluring notions, Stendhal acquires literary practice in his *Journal*. This diary, often disappointing in its adolescent and dandyish self-centeredness, is of particular interest for the years 1804–1805, a period of insecurity and intense self-trial. Jean Prévost very aptly calls this period "the apprenticeship of interior discourse." [3] The young would-be writer and lover, always prone to be both his own patient and diagnostician, indulges in endless consultations, tortures himself with thorough examinations of vexing episodes, raises questions, provides answers and advice, and engages in a dialogue with himself that clearly suggests one of the basic tenets of Beylisme: the ethics of self-esteem.

His drawn-out, clumsy amorous strategy to seduce the only too-willing actress Mélanie Guilbert is the subject of almost fictionally structured episodes in his diary. The two met in the acting classes of Dugazon, under the very sign of impersonation. While reciting French classics with her, Stendhal became, in his own eyes, the actor of a self-staged plot of seduction in which he constantly watched and appraised his own performance. The *Journal* details these amorous maneuvers, this characteristic view of love as an almost military enterprise. These pages cast light on the particular tensions of Stendhalian love as revealed in his novels, specifically on the thematic value of projected future action. Stendhal was indeed always to conceive of love as a battle. "Histoire *de la bataille du 31 mai 1811*"—

these words mark the beginning of a later section of his diary. But it is a battle in which the hero-strategist will be successful in directly reverse proportion to the intensity of his emotions. Hence the poetry of defeat. The *Journal* represents not only an important stage in the Stendhalian apprenticeship in the inversion of values, but also a growing tendency to view himself as his own "character." It is not surprising that, rereading a passage in 1819, Stendhal is led to speak of himself as "that man": "Cet homme est à jeter par les fenêtres." [4]

The awareness of the self in a dramatic continuum is probably the most valuable experience the future novelist derived from the practice of keeping a diary. Similarly, hindsight enables us to attribute a formative value to the hybrid literary enterprises in which he indulged between 1814 and 1826. *Rome, Naples et Florence en 1817*, his first literary success, is a curious mixture of travelogue, fictional diary, survey of the musical life of Italy, political and sociological insights, topical anecdotes, and dilettantish pleasure seeking. Behind it all, behind the mask of the music-loving cavalry officer with a reassuring Germanic pseudonym, the book is a subversive pamphlet. The ironic disclaimers and aggressive paradoxes serve only to underscore the criticism of the victorious reactionary political order in Italy and in Europe after Napoleon's fall. Such, without a question, was Stendhal's aim in writing this incisive book. But the very paradoxes and ambiguities that he cultivates here also read like an early rehearsal of the peculiar counterpoint of satire and tenderness, of lyricism and lucid irony, that makes up the texture of his novels. For *Rome, Naples et Florence* blends art and politics, the cult of sensations and the passion for debunking, indignation and the chronic ability to

admire and feel enthusiasm. In this volume, as in his beloved opera buffa, the *recitativo secco* and the tender aria
alternate: satire is flirting here with the theme of happiness, as moral judgment and esthetic preferences are
brought into unlikely coexistence. This ambivalence of
tone and meaning extends to the central themes of political and psychological freedom.

The digressive *Histoire de la peinture en Italie* (1817),
though neither an authentic history of painting nor an
entirely original work, contains a wealth of provocative
esthetic notions: on modernity, on the importance of temperament and geographic climate, on ideal beauty. The
Introduction is a model of irrelevance and brio. Baudelaire
admired the book's insights and sallies, though art histori-
ans have been justifiably baffled. But it too is primarily a
pamphlet; descriptions of paintings are often mere pretexts for social and political observations or innuendoes. In
fact, all these early texts betray a true political and polem-
ical passion. Even *Racine et Shakespeare,* a double pamphlet in favor of Romanticism and the emancipation from
the rigid rules of Academic writing, is rich in political
implications. This passion for politics was to prove one of
the most powerful inspirations for his novels. He repeatedly quipped that the intrusion of politics in fiction was as
incongruous as a pistol shot in a concert hall. Yet he suspected that this incongruity led to a deeper truth. "One
cannot, in the midst of the revolution that grips us, study
the mores of a people without indulging in politics," he
observed in *Rome, Naples et Florence.* The Revolution
had begun in 1789; but Stendhal knew that it was far
from over. His so-called realism lies not in a photographic
fidelity to detail, but in the intuition that no individual
destiny could, in this tormented era, be separated from the

events and forces that determine it. As novelist, repeatedly, he was to welcome the pistol shot.

Stendhal's extreme sensitivity to the currents and cross-currents of contemporary history had been sharpened by his frequent encounters with Liberals and Carbonari in Milan. His relations with men such as Ludovico di Breme and Silvio Pellico, who was soon to languish in the Spielberg prison, had compromised him forever with the Austrian authorities. This fascination with politics was put to use and further heightened by Stendhal's journalistic activities after his return to Paris. From 1822 to 1827, he earned about two hundred pounds a year—perhaps two-thirds of his income—by contributing anonymous articles to English publications such as *Paris Monthly Review, Athenaeum, New Monthly Magazine, London Magazine.* Many such contributions are probably still buried in various English journals; the ones that have been identified fill five volumes of the *Courrier anglais,* edited by Henri Martineau. It would be wrong, however, to view these articles as a mere by-product or as a purely alimentary exercise. Ever since his Milanese friends acquainted him with the *Edinburgh Review* (a great event in his life), it became his ambition to collaborate with this, or with some other English review. And although he occasionally flattered English prejudices (his statements on Napoleon, for instance, should be taken with several grains of salt), anonymity as well as publication outside of France encouraged his outspokenness on intellectual, social, and political matters.

Stendhal was unusually well informed. One of his intimate friends, the Baron de Mareste, headed a department at the Préfecture de Police. Another friend, Joseph Lingay, was confidential secretary to the Minister of the Interior, Decazes. The Sunday afternoon gatherings of Romantic Liberals in the salon of Delécluze were for him a mine of information. He was, moreover, an avid newspaper reader: the *Journal des Débats, Le Globe, Le Constitutionnel*, the reactionary *La Quotidienne* and *Le Moniteur*, whatever Stendhal's hostility to their tone or attitudes, provided him with facts or opinions. His own articles, destined for English consumption, are a brisk, though often partial chronicle of political and intellectual life in France under the Restoration. Some of the book reviews, including a self-promoting article on his own *Racine et Shakespeare*, are amusing. His reactions to Hugo's wild imagination in *Han d'Islande* make for savory reading. But it is the political chronicle and the shrewd political diagnoses that take on special interest.

The *Courrier anglais* reveals a mind unusually well attuned to the key events of this Revolutionary period: the counteroffensive of the *ultras* after the murder of the Duke of Berri, the second Richelieu ministry, the passing of the new electoral law favoring landed proprietors, of the Law of Indemnity compensating nobles for losses during the Revolution, of the Law of Sacrilege imposing the death penalty for certain offenses of a so-called sacrilegious nature. The Villèle ministry in particular had undertaken the impossible task of setting the clock back to pre-Revolutionary days. During these anachronistic and oppressive years, Stendhal learned no doubt more about the laws of history than during the entire Napoleonic adventure. This lesson was to feed the pungent satire of *Le Rouge et le Noir* as well as the comic and burlesque fantasy of *La Chartreuse de Parme*. But even though it found its expression in irony or parody, the lesson was serious.

What Stendhal undertakes for his English readers is a

critical tableau of French social and political mores. He evokes the three different types of aristocracies (the *ultras* of the Faubourg Saint-Germain, the Liberal group represented by Saint-Aulaire and Moglie, the moneyed aristocracy of the Chaussée d'Antin), the boredom and insignificance of court life, the submissiveness of an army obedient to any master, the subservience of a magistrature eager to please the nobility. He is at his keenest when conjuring up a busy and plotting clergy, which is dominated by the Jesuits, preparing for civil war and teaching their peasant-seminarists the use of firearms.[5] Julien Sorel was soon to encounter these lazy and venal young peasants in the Besançon seminary. The contrasts that Stendhal establishes in the *Courrier anglais* between the highly centralized Parisian life and the soporific existence in the provinces, so propitious to feminine reveries, also prefigure a central theme of the novel, which, without his knowing, was beginning to take shape in his mind.

Stendhal's remarks are not limited to briskly related anecdotes or to incisive conclusions. Behind the rapid sketches and the censorious vein, one detects a troubled and at the same time exhilarated awareness of the acceleration of history. He observes that the Frenchman of 1824 is a totally different creature from the subject of Louis XV, that a man of sixty has ideas irreconcilable with those of his thirty-year-old son.[6] Repeatedly, he stresses the co-existence of several generations, very close to one another in time, but hopelessly estranged by divergent education and experience. Stendhal's novels vividly dramatize this theme of clashing generations. Fathers and sons, even brothers, have become alienated from one another.

The drama of contemporary history looms in the background of all of Stendhal's writings, chiefly his novels. He was perhaps the first European writer to sense so clearly the uselessness of inherited values for solving ever new problems. The political upheavals that occurred during his life span (the death of the Ancien Régime, the Directory, the Consulate, the Empire, the military debacle, the Restoration, the July Monarchy) convinced him of the impossibility of any political entrenchment. As for history, it could no longer be a gratuitous archaeological enterprise, a form of tourism into the past. It had become an explosive force, the modern manifestation of necessity, a *fatum*, to which man was both the victimized subject and the necessary midwife.

In terms of the drama of contemporary history and of the critical awareness of political events, the *Courrier anglais*, with its broad range of topics, was an excellent preparation, almost a dress rehearsal for his novels. One other text, totally unlike anything he had written so far, marks his gradual transition from polemicist and literary dilettante to novelist.

De l'Amour (1822), a book that brings Stendhal closest to fiction, is also the most "personal" text published during his lifetime. No wonder that, in a striking chapter only four lines long, Stendhal asks himself with some anxiety whether he succeeded in silencing a heart that wishes to speak out. "I fear that I have written down but a sigh, when I think that I have noted a truth." For *De l'Amour*, on the surface an ideological essay that explicitly threatens to treat the alluring subject of love "simply, reasonably and mathematically," is in fact simultaneously a sentimental justification, a self-administered therapeutic treatment, and a Stendhalian *Vita Nuova*. Stendhal's Beatrice is the proud Milanese lady Métilde Dembowski, who refused his love, who exiled him from her salon, and whose memory was to haunt him for the rest of his life. There is no doubt that this intelligent but easily offended woman became one of the lasting inspirations for the novelist.

De l'Amour is often cited for its so-called theories on the most important of human avocations: the four different types of love, the seven stages in its development leading up to the famous "crystallization," the relation between climate, political institution, temperament, and the art of loving. Yet it is the thinly veiled personal confession —not love in general, but specific and unrequited love— that lends this book its deeper resonance. The transposition is obvious: Stendhal becomes his own confidant, as he both deprecates and justifies himself, perhaps faintly hoping that the inaccessible Métilde herself might read the book and be moved. This emotional, or emotion-producing tendency constantly brings this curious book to the very threshold of fiction. "Voyage into an Unknown Country" is the title of one of the chapters dramatizing the figure of Lisio Visconti who experiences the unbearable fever of waiting for his beloved, suffers from acute crises of self-consciousness when in her company, and punishes himself for his own humiliations. The disguise is transparent. Visconti is of course Stendhal himself; and so is Salviati, who is rejected by the woman he desperately loves, accused of indelicacy, and condemned to a regimen of two monthly visits. The almost delirious clumsiness during these rare visits, the further harm he does himself in the woman's eyes, self-recrimination and self-consolation—all this describes in fact Stendhal's own tortures in love. But this acute personal experience is already in the process of being transmuted into a fictional construct.

Perhaps nothing better suggests this creative metamorphosis of lived experience within the texture of *De l'Amour* than Stendhal's tendency to supply imaginary compensations. A binocular vision repeatedly provides, for the very same event or experience, the emotions of the involved character as well as the understanding and interpretation of an all-knowing author. On the simplest level, these compensatory optics imply an excellence in amorous suffering and in amorous failure. Stendhal thus prefers the bitter happiness of Werther to the sterile success of Don Juan. Werther, according to Stendhal, cultivates his inefficacy and his defeats as proof of his sensibility and as a source of deeper joys. In a chapter appropriately entitled "Werther et Don Juan," he denounces the "sécheresse" of the seducer and maintains that the unhappy lover, though not exactly a prestigious figure in society, is initiated, through his very suffering, into the realm of emotional and artistic beauty.

On a deeper level, the need for compensations leads to experiments with unrealized, hypothetical situations. The creative imagination is here fully at work: Stendhal conceives of hidden victories, which the timid lover is too blind to observe and too clumsy to exploit—semivictories of which the almost defeated woman is herself only partially aware. Did she love? This is the overwhelming question Stendhal ceaselessly asks himself after the Milanese adventure. It is the same question that haunts his heroes and to which they, or rather their author, provide a circuitous but unequivocally affirmative answer. In *De l'Amour,* there is the repeated intimation that Métilde did not dare to love, that it was her feminine modesty—her *pudeur* or self-conscious fear in the face of her own emotions—that acted as the most powerful restraint. Stendhal puts down on paper this revealing observation: "A woman is capable of loving, and, in an entire year, of saying no

more than ten or twelve words to the man she prefers."
There is also the intimation that the lover is too busy loving to be aware of his victory: "I have seen a man discover
that his rival was loved, and the latter not see it because of
his passion." Assuaging reveries such as these lead Stendhal directly to fiction, and account for the delicate interweaving of the themes of blindness, self-esteem, and
freedom in his novels.

Analysis and lyricism are the twin poles of *De l'Amour*.
But it is the tender and musical element that predominates. The deviation from the pseudoscientific beginning
to the poetry of passion is indeed so marked that the ideological pages ultimately function as counterpoint and protective façade. In fact, *De l'Amour* is a mine of evocative,
highly personal notations on crystallization, on love as a
fever and a flirtation with peril, on revery and the impossibility of any musical transcription of its joys, on the poetry of incommunicability. "The revery of love cannot be
set down." Yet some of the most successful passages—one
should say moments—of *De l'Amour* are fleeting but
acute resurrections of privileged instants. "Ave Maria
(twilight), in Italy the hour of tenderness, of the pleasures of the soul and of melancholy: sensation increased by
the sound of these beautiful bells." Rousseau proves to be
a more meaningful and more lasting influence on Stendhal than Helvétius. *De l'Amour* thus combines daydream scenes and fantasies of wish-fulfillment with the
poetry of associations and of memory. The two trends
merge into the specifically Stendhalian poetry of fiction.

A number of texts mark Stendhal's gradual evolution
toward the novel and his apprenticeship *malgré lui*. In

Pensées. Filosofia Nova, the newly converted adolescent disciple of Ideology wrestles with freshly acquired lessons in analysis and energy. In the *Journal,* he practices self-questioning and creates dramatic situations into which he casts himself both as subject and project. That he eagerly indulged in literary exercises is evidenced by the "Caractères," those psychological portraits undertaken in 1805 in collaboration with his friend Louis Crozet. These factual assessments and unidealized dissections, often studded with crude details, were not meant for publication. The models are drawn from real life—many of them colleagues of the engineer Crozet—without any attempt at disguise. Thus we learn that one Derrien is stocky, ready to laugh, that he stands in awe of good clothes, is proud of his teeth, which he cleans twice a day, and is in love with a slut. These analytical sketches, whose professed purpose is the superior insight into "le coeur humain," held a special appeal for the would-be playwright who was more interested by far in the drama of character than in the drama of situation. But the genre of the "portrait" and of the "caractère," rooted in the tradition of the seventeenth-century French "moralistes," had been a particularly fecund influence on the eighteenth-century novel, specifically on the novel of manners or of worldliness.[7] Stendhal's analytic taste and his practice in these early texts led him to the literary genre most hospitable to analysis and most susceptible to development in that direction: the novel.

The mania for self-examination and strategy appears most clearly in an amusing and revealing text entitled *Consultation pour Banti* (1811). Banti was but another among the many assumed pseudonyms. As for the "Consultation," it concerns the possibilities and timeliness of seducing Mme Daru, the wife of one of Napoleon's most gifted administrators who was the Parisian protector of young Henri. The text characteristically begins with a question: "Must I or must I not have the duchess?" Stendhal was fond of these consultations, in which he could simultaneously act out the parts of patient and of omniscient diagnostician. He proceeds to examine his chances, plans a course of action, and applies the lessons of Ideology according to which *connaître* and *pénétrer* are almost interchangeable. Analysis here is a function of conquest. But it is also a function of fantasy and of fictional invention. There is something frankly juvenile about such a text, yet the character study of the Duchess de Bérulle (Countess Daru) is nuanced and complex. It takes into account her formative years, the influence of her mother, her religious training, her fondness for dancing, her capacity for passion, her reactions to joy and misfortune, her basic beliefs, her probable demands on a lover, her attitude toward her children, her inhibitions. It is, in other words, a miniature biography and portrait. Stendhal even sketches the character of her husband. Most interesting, however, are the hypothetical situations he creates. How will she succumb to love? Stendhal invents a dramatic scene: "She will be carried away, in a moment of weakness, out in the country, during the summer, at eight o'clock in the evening, two hours after a good dinner during which she will have talked a lot." [8] One almost imagines Julien with Madame de Rênal in the garden of Vergy. The miniature portrait has turned into a miniature novel.

Stendhal's talent for story telling was also given practice in his early nonfictional writings. The tragic love of Bianca Capello as told in *Histoire de la peinture en Italie* reads like an early version of any one of the "Chroniques italiennes," complete with secret signals, elopement, jealousy, murder, and suicide. This delight in digressive stories and in elaborate anecdotes is more striking if one compares Stendhal's text with that of his sources, which he so frequently plagiarizes. The account of the monk Fra Filippo Lippi's love for his model Lucrezia Buti, a convent seduction in which passion first speaks the secret language of the eyes, is clearly a dramatic and colorful account by a potential novelist.[9] In *Rome, Naples et Florence,* the technique of a fictional diary introduces from the start elements of narrative construction and novelistic texture, which are further intensified by the creation of fictional situations, character portraits, dramatic chance meetings, stories of desperate passions, cruel deeds, and generous brigands, and by a steady effort to bring out characteristic and picturesque details. On occasion, the notion of a novel almost seems to force itself into Stendhal's consciousness. Speaking of a Bolognese lady, he adds that her life "ferait un des romans les plus intéressants . . ."[10] The image of Duchess Sanseverina clearly began to haunt Stendhal many years before he finally gave her an exalted role in *La Chartreuse de Parme.*

The biographical approach, in the case of Stendhal, cannot be neglected. The experience of falling in love with Métilde Dembowski in 1818 (Stendhal himself called it the "beginning of a long musical phrase") and the distressing inability to find his way into her heart had a lasting effect on his creative imagination and brought about intensive, self-punishing, and compensatory rumination. One could point to some striking resemblances between letters written to the Milanese lady in 1819 and passages in *Lucien Leuwen,* composed in 1834. Stendhal was in fact perfectly aware that he was rediscovering and even deciphering the past as he wrote about Lucien's love for Mme de Chasteller. At a twenty-five-year interval, one finds the same complaints, the same justifications, even the same expressions. It is almost as though he consulted the drafts or copies of his old letters. But the pain of the experience and the humiliations of the memory are here transmuted into the joy of creation. Stendhal himself was surprised by the affective proximity and intensity of past emotions. "I write upon the sensations of 1819," he confides in his droll English to the margin of his manuscript, in the passage where Lucien finds consolation in drink.

The two early texts that most clearly testify to the literary importance of his sentimental experiences and mark the final evolution toward the novel are the curious pages known as *Le Roman de Métilde*[11] and the brief illustrative tale, or imaginary case history, entitled *Ernestine ou la naissance de l'amour*. *Le Roman de Métilde* (1819), or rather simply *Roman* as Stendhal called it, is an eleven-page fictional confession destined to move Métilde Dembowski and convince her of the purity and delicacy of his love. Fiction was to serve as intercessor. The novelette, written in four hours during an outburst of hope, was, however, never completed and never sent. But the motivation behind its composition, the situation described, and above all the sketch of the protagonist are of great interest to the student of Stendhal. The lover, Poloski, a Polish officer who had served under Napoleon, can neither hide nor adequately express his love. Clumsy and jealous, he suffers almost as much from his own inadequacies as from the indifference of Countess Bianca. This Italian beauty with a melancholy and imposing Lombard profile carries the nobility of a tragic temperament and a spiritual grace invisible to the vulgar eye. Another character, the Duchess of Empoli, a haughty and possessive friend of Bianca, stands in the way of Poloski. This hostile type, probably drawn after Métilde's cousin Mme Traversi, appears several times in Stendhal's novels. But the most interesting personage in *Le Roman de Métilde* is no doubt Baron Zanca, Poloski's worldly-wise, cynical friend, who is for him a confidant, an external judge, and a cruelly objective denigrator of his seductive talents. For the fictional impulse, with Stendhal, combines the need for communication and consolation with the bitter pleasures of lucidity and self-derision.

The other text that carries Stendhal to the threshold of the novel, *Ernestine ou la naissance de l'amour,* appears as an Appendix to *De l'Amour.* Its point of departure is a sentence of Chapter 4 that plots the various stages of love, which, from availability and surprise, lead to admiration, hope, and crystallization. Stendhal imagines the sentiments of a lonely young girl, living with an old uncle in an isolated château, who falls in love with a stranger-huntsman. The degrees by which she becomes aware of her love and admits this love to herself are most delicately suggested. The tone is at times clearly "demonstrative." But, almost in spite of the author, the demonstration gives way to narration and analysis, as fictional techniques gain the upper hand. The rhythm of the narration, the occasional use of a dramatic present tense, the obvious concern for creating and maintaining suspense, all indicate the pleasure with which the author develops his "theoretical" story. Stendhal himself even seems aware that it leads him in the direction of the novel. "I could write ten volumes like Richardson . . ."; ". . . I do not have the space to write a novel." But in fact, the illustrative Appendix to *De l'Amour* is some twenty-five pages long, and does leave ample room for descriptions, psychological tensions, interior monologues, dramatic situations, and even satire. More important still, *Ernestine ou la naissance de l'amour* clearly proposes some fundamental Stendhalian themes, which will be fully developed in the later novels: the unawareness, or partial blindness, of the protagonist; her *pudeur* and self-deprecation; the author's fondness for his character in moments of weakness and inadequacy; the painful consciousness of the glance of the "other," the desire to be seen and yet to avoid exposure. Love is viewed not as a clinical reality, but as a fragile creation that can survive only where there also exists the most exquisite quality of soul.

ARMANCE: *FREEDOM AND SELF-ESTEEM*

Stendhal's hesitations on the road to fiction seem confirmed by the fact that *Armance* is indirectly the result of a literary hoax. It is as though Stendhal needed the pretense of a game to indulge openly in what turned out to be for him a serious matter indeed. The circumstances are by now well known: Mme de Duras, who specialized in novels of social or emotional impossibilities (*Ourika, Edouard*), had written a book in 1825 about a sexually impotent hero whose physical deficiency represented the greatest of all possible obstacles to love. Only the title of

this work, *Olivier ou le secret,* was known to the public;
the subject was apparently too delicate. Mme de Duras
died a few years later without publishing the novel. But
private readings or indiscretion brought the story to the
attention of Henri de Latouche, who achieved a *succès de
scandale* by writing and publishing anonymously, in exactly the same format and with the same typography as
Mme de Duras' novels, an *Olivier* of his own. This game
of mystification titillated Stendhal, who, some months
later, conceived the idea of writing a novel about a "ba-
bilan" or sexually inadequate hero, originally named Olivier.[12] But interest in the scandal had waned; the literary
joke had become stale. *Armance* brought Stendhal
enough money to make a trip to Italy, but did nothing for
his literary reputation.

It is tempting to speculate on what, besides the game,
attracted Stendhal to such a subject. Sexual "fiascos" already interested him at the time he wrote *De l'Amour;* an
entire chapter is devoted to this scabrous topic. But "babilanism" was another matter. In a crude letter to Mérimée
(23 December 1826), invaluable because it casts light on
his intentions and on the implications of a subject never
explicitly treated in the novel, he clearly expresses his interest in the physiological and psychological problem
raised by chronic or congenital impotence. But it seemed
likely that, from the start, the subject and the psychological type appealed to him because of the possible exploitation of the theme of alienation. Octave, the hero of *Armance,* is indeed a stranger, not only to love (though in
love), but to the society to which he belongs. He is both
in and *out,* a participant and an observer, active and condemned to lucid passivity.

It is remarkable indeed that Stendhal waited until September 1826 to pick up an idea he had had almost a year earlier, especially if his sole intention was to join in the game of deception, which by then could no longer possibly be timely. Other motives must have impelled him. "Repris comme remède le 19 septembre 1826 . . ." he cryptically explains in a marginal note.[13] But what was this a remedy for? A quick glance at the events of that year explains the need for literary therapy. In May 1826, Countess Clémentine Curial, after two years of a passionate and stormy affair, signified to him that all was over, that she was in love with someone else. This "affreux malheur," as Stendhal himself referred to the event, almost drove him to suicide. *Armance* was begun soon after under the sign of despair.

Despair may have been the immediate cause for the resumption of the project (literary work functioning as a derivative from pain); it certainly colors the tone of the novel. But personal suffering remains strangely external to the subject of the book and to its themes. No adequate fusion or correspondence seems to have been established between Stendhal's private concerns and the dilemmas of his hero. The experience and the vision of the author remain extrinsic to the character's predicament. One may accept the author's formulations of Octave's condition; these formulations are often nuanced and elegantly terse. Yet the causes and motivations for the alternate crises of apathy and enthusiasm remain obscure. A thinness of texture and a fundamental lack of proportion vitiate the novel, not so much because the author deprives the reader of a key to Octave's secret "babilanism," but because he transfers to his protagonist the private intensity of recent memories and a despondency whose sources are not rooted in the specific plight of the impotent young hero. *Ar-*

mance, as a result, suffers from a certain fuzziness, a mysterious lack of focus, and a blurred perspective, which are, however, not without charm.

Part of the difficulty lies in Stendhal's lack of talent for plot construction. Left to his own devices, he was strangely ungifted for conceiving a dramatic, or even logical, concatenation of events. He thus, more or less arbitrarily, confronts his two main characters, Octave and his cousin Armance, with a series of unpredictable obstacles. In fact, *obstacle,* as a technical device, evidently inherited from his meditations on dramaturgy,[14] is almost elevated to the dignity of a theme. The long-range consequences of this obstacle technique were destined to be far-reaching. Stendhal came to exploit the obstacle, not as a dramatic tool for suspense and the rebounding of action, but as a moral and emotional *test.* All of Stendhal's heroes are thus exposed, and zestfully expose themselves, to the maximum number of trials.

As it stands, the plot of *Armance* turns around the scruples of a hero who is afraid to love and yet afraid to lose the esteem of the cousin he loves, and the equally involved scruples of a young girl who, ashamed of her own emotions, prefers not to be loved to falling in the esteem and losing the respect of the young man she loves. A choreography of pride is at the center of the book. The setting is the Restoration society. The love of the two oversusceptible protagonists is situated in the midst of the stuffiness and boredom of aristocratic salons. Politics, in the form of the Law of Indemnity compensating nobles for losses of land during the Revolution, provides a major element of tension. Do two million francs go to Octave's head? Do two million francs transform Armance into a schemer maneuvering to marry for money? The question is never objectively asked. The characters' doubts are entirely subjective and are not experienced by the reader. Even worse than these doubts about the "other" are doubts about the self. "Ah! que je me déplais à moi-même! . . ." (Chapter 3) To deserve one's own contempt is probably the most distressing, and also the most endearing trait of the Stendhalian hero.

Byronic undertones make Octave a hero of his time. After the marriage, which cannot be consummated, he flees to Greece, pretending that he vowed to fight there. His escape is not only from the marriage bed but from life, as though life itself were a curse. On the ship's deck, in sight of the Greek shore, he commits suicide and dies a poetic death with a smile on his lips. These Byronic elements are further stressed by the hero's somber moods and crises of violence. Stendhal was soon to give up this Romantic pose for which he had in fact little patience.

A case could no doubt be made to show that Stendhal was keenly aware of the sexual pathology involved, that although he did not care to discuss these matters explicitly, the behavior of Octave at every point offers almost medical symptoms and symbols. Thus Georges Blin undertakes a "pathological exegesis," talks of "neurosis" and of "syndromes," and invokes Pinel, Freud, and learned works of psychopathology.[15] There is no doubt that Stendhal was acquainted with Pinel's *Traité médico-philosophique sur l'aliénation mentale ou la manie,* as well as with Cabanis' work on the relation between physical and psychological factors. But it is easy to exaggerate the sexual symbolism of the book and its pathological accuracy. It would seem, on the contrary, that Stendhal underplayed these elements, and that he disregarded the physiological causes of Octave's disturbed psyche not because of deli-

cacy or prudence, but simply because the real subject of
the book lay elsewhere.

The original subtitle of *Armance*, "Anecdote du XIXe
siècle," unequivocally states the historical orientation of
the novel. The author's intentions must be set against the
background of his political and broadly cultural curiosity
displayed in the journalistic pieces collected in the *Courrier anglais*. The publisher convinced him to use the even
more specific subtitle "Quelques scènes d'un salon de
Paris en 1827." In *Armance*, Stendhal indeed hoped to
provide, if not a complete and colorful tableau, at least an
incisive pen drawing of the decadent Parisian aristocracy.
He explicitly refers, in a brief intervention in Chapter 29,
to the "gangrened products of the new generation." The
trouble is that Stendhal did not have firsthand knowledge
of the aristocratic salons of the Faubourg Saint-Germain.
Hence an additional element of vagueness in the novel.

Impotence, in this instance, is not merely an individual's physiological deficiency, but the hidden symbol of
the shameful deterioration of an entire social class. Class
consciousness and class criticism, though of a diagnostic
rather than a militant nature, are indeed prominent in
Stendhal's work, and constitute one of the most original
contributions of his novels. If one can speak of Stendhal's
"realism," it is not because of any obsession with physical
setting, costumes, or material details of daily life, but because of a permanent concern with the underlying historical, political, and economic currents of his time. This constant awareness of a sociopolitical background is what
makes this minor novel a milestone in the history of literary realism. *Armance*, preceding Balzac's first major novels
by several years, rings a new note.

Another typically Stendhalian feature is the double

judgment involved. Octave sees and judges the defects of his class; but Octave himself is judged and criticized. The ironically viewed ironic hero—Stendhal's specific contribution to the development of the "unheroic hero" in nineteenth-century literature—is a major source of ambiguity in his novels. But these ambiguities, disconcerting to the hasty or unsophisticated reader, point to a relativistic perspective that transcends the specific work of Stendhal. *Armance* could not have been written thirty years earlier, though it may appear in many ways quite conventional in tone and even slightly dated in flavor. Its ambivalences and implicit relativism reflect the spirit of an age that was taking stock of its instability and of the impossibility of continuing to live on anachronistic values. The esthetic and moral consequences of this "demythification" are complex and of the utmost importance. Stendhal himself, in *Souvenirs d'égotisme,* proclaims that "le génie du soupçon" would henceforth dominate the world. This new era of "suspicion" allowed little room, if any, for naïve lyricism or invariable principles. All was now subject to examination; nothing could be taken for granted. The problem of moral freedom is thus implicit in the mobility and disquietude of the author's point of view. If the traditional hero has become an impossibility, it is because values have become fluid, and moral codes uncertain. But if external rules cannot be trusted, if society has become the great counterfeiter, then the individual must work out his own rules of conduct. Integrity, for Stendhal, becomes a matter of self-respect. The relativistic perspective, far from encouraging cynicism or surrender, brings about self-discipline and compels the Stendhalian hero to forge his own rigorous moral code. Freedom and self-esteem have been joined, and pride—that *amour-propre* so abhorrent to Pascal—has paradoxically become the instrument for an ethical quest.

The themes of *Armance* clearly take priority over its subject. Octave and Armance discover that it is more difficult not to look down on oneself than it is to seek favor in the opinion of others. The shame of loving, the self-made and self-kept pacts, the thirst for lucidity, the taste for dissimulation, and the dreams of circulating "incognito" ("j'ai soif de l'*incognito*")—all this suggests a solipsistic moral experience. To see himself as though he were "another" is Octave's explicit desire. He does not seek this otherness in order to elude himself, but to better appraise his merits and shortcomings. *Armance* is Stendhal's first fictional elaboration of the themes of self-discipline and self-imposed morality. The obstacles are not so much arbitrarily introduced by the author as required by the protagonists—for self-protection, but also for self-probation. The notion of the obstacle is indeed part and parcel of the Stendhalian glorification of gratuitous duty. But it is gratuitousness, even more than duty, that attracts him. The quest for personal morality and the latent hostility to social rules thus transcend a peevish misanthropy or a naïve Romantic rebellion against the arch-enemy, society. This quest and this hostility symbolize nostalgia for moral and psychological freedom.

The narrative techniques in *Armance*—though often clumsy—also bring out the fundamental theme of freedom. Stendhal makes his own presence felt through direct interventions and an abundant use of maxim-like observations, very much in the tradition of Mme de Lafayette, Mme de Souza, or Mme de Genlis. *La Princesse de Clèves* was, in fact, Stendhal's touchstone as he composed

Armance. These maxims communicate wordly wisdom, moral judgments, psychological truths, and esthetic appreciations. They are part of that general system of intrusions that Stendhal inherited from his predecessors, but which he very originally exploits for his own ends. For it is clear that the narrative presence of the author cannot be attributed solely to habit, caprice, or the impertinent desire to make himself heard. His ironic observations, his approvals and apologies, and his frequent private little discussions with his reader cannot be taken for mere histrionic manifestations. For side by side with the need to appropriate his own tale and to make it correspond to his intimate preoccupations, Stendhal also feels an equally strong urge to detach himself, to express his lack of solidarity. He thus plays the role of repudiator who seemingly disavows and even betrays his own creation.[16]

Stendhal intrudes into *Armance* on almost every page. The young protagonists are judged from an adult and experienced viewpoint; their inability to understand life, each other, and themselves is repeatedly stressed. Stendhal constantly interrupts his characters and asserts his own personal tastes and opinions. This usurpation is so habitual, the transitions from the characters' consciousness to that of the author are so swift, that the reader, after a while, hardly notices the changes in perspective. Moreover, almost all the author's direct commentaries are charged with ambiguity. Stendhal assumes a paternal attitude, now haughty, now benevolent. He underscores the naïveté of Octave and takes an almost malicious pleasure in revealing his defects and weaknesses. Stendhal even presents qualities he obviously valued (Octave's contempt for his caste, his insubordination to silly conventions, his intolerance for sham and cant, his exalted sense of personal dignity) through mockeries and almost in the guise of blame.

Nothing is more characteristic of Stendhal's oblique approach than the equivocal juggling of the notions of blame and praise. And nothing is more revealing of his art and of his temperament than the habit of underlining through sarcasm precisely those passages that present the hero at his romantic best. This irony not only protects that which he holds most dear (whether feelings or illusions), but allows his characters the maximum amount of freedom possible within the conventions of fiction. The very presence of the self-assertive author reacting to the happenings of his story seems to guarantee the independence of his creatures.

Yet *Armance* remains, despite its subtle sadness, nuanced perspectives, and original exploitations of narrative convention, a disappointing novel. Its irresoluteness and fuzziness are largely due to the absence of a proper "objective correlative." What is missing, in fact, is the synthesis of memory and imagination. Stendhal—as his later works prove—could achieve this fusion only when he was free from the concerns of plot construction, that is, when he was carried by preexistent external events. Only in the presence of such an external necessity, whether in the form of an Italian chronicle or of the newspaper account of a crime, did he feel free to unfold his inner plot. The result accounts for the extraordinary coexistence and counterpoint of an inner and an outer reality in Stendhal's best novels. The intensity of *Le Rouge et le Noir* is in large measure the result of this paradoxical interplay of plot necessity and the freedom to dream.

3

LE ROUGE ET LE NOIR

the Ambiguities of Freedom

Approaches

Stendhal himself guides us into the novel: we enter the provincial town of Verrières together with a Parisian traveler-narrator. This tourist beginning, with its description of white houses, red tiles, and opulent chestnut trees, is not gratuitous. Through the eyes of the sophisticated Parisian itinerant, we survey, with apparent detachment, a setting to which we are not invited to belong. The transient nature of the arrival suggests mental mobility and ironic distance. The presence of the foreign observer introduces, from the very start, an intermediary voice between the events of the book and the reader. The specific perspective is that of the outsider. But the device also establishes, proleptically, the two geographic and moral poles of the novel: Paris and the Provinces. Indeed, the Parisian tourist is more involved than he might at first appear to be. The irony is two-edged, and ultimately cancels itself out. Already in the first pages of the novel, savoir-faire and worldly experience discredit themselves. As the amused and hypothetical "Parisian" glimpses Madame de Rênal, the connoisseur in him immediately conjures up libertine visions. Yet Madame de Rênal's "naïve grace" and total lack of coquetry would be quite inconceivable in the unspontaneous, unnatural, and devitalized world of Paris.

The antithesis of city and nature is at first developed within the provincial context. Verrières, with its constricting walls and petty commercial concerns, is surrounded by splendid mountains. Upon entering the town, one immediately hears the horrible din of a nail factory. The machine "of terrifying aspect" with twenty heavy hammers is serviced by pretty young girls who appear like slaves of the voracious monster of industry. The contrast between the strident mechanism and the delicate human figures conveys the notion of an inhuman ceremony. Nature is being brutalized and profaned by the ogre of mercantilism. The image of these frail young hands exposed to the blows of the hammers serves as an initial commentary on social values that in Stendhal's view have dehumanized modern man. But it also serves to introduce the owner of the factory, the mayor of Verrières, M. de Rênal. His vulgar materialism, as well as the plight of a woman forced by marriage to tolerate his loud, obtrusive presence, is symbolized by the image of the deafening factory.

The casual, ambling beginning is studded with symbolic details. The gardens in Verrières are locked in by jealous and possessive walls. Trees are cut, clipped, and pruned in a barbaric manner. What is suggested is not merely a utilitarian spirit of conformity, but the steady repression of nature. Stendhal explicitly compares these amputated plants to the "splendid shapes" of English plane trees left to grow unhampered. What adds significance to these arboreal observations is Stendhal's habit of comparing a vigorous humanity (for instance, the dynamic men of the Renaissance) to a powerful and exuberant vegetation. To clip trees is to deprive them of their individuality; it is in fact a form of emasculation. This reduction to humiliating conformity symbolizes the pervasive tyranny of inhibitions and servile social conventions.

The theme of freedom introduced in the second paragraph by the *topos* of the mountain is developed by other images of verticality. When we first see Julien Sorel in the shed of the sawmill, which he is supposed to supervise, he is sitting five or six feet high, astride one of the rafters of the roof. His position "à cheval" is of course in harmony with the book he is reading, his beloved *Mémorial de Sainte-Hélène*. The altitude is physical, to be sure, but intellectual (his reading of books infuriates his illiterate father) and emotional as well. His imagination carries him high above the concerns of his axe-wielding brothers to the epic and mythic realm of Napoleon's exploits. The translation of spiritual exaltation into ascensional images occurs again, at the end of Chapter 10, in almost Rousseauistic terms, when Julien, to "see clearly in his own soul," climbs the rocky mountain and feels a lofty separation from ordinary humanity. Stendhal is quite explicit: the sense of height corresponds symbolically to the "position he was burning to attain in the moral sphere." The expressions "pure air," "serenity," and "joy" indicate the spirit in which the episode must be read. The immense panorama, the hawk describing large circles over his head, the inebriating silence and isolation—all contribute to the theme of victorious elevation above the choking realities of Verrières.

The novel clearly offers from the start a complex thematic structure. Point of view and images suggest a mobile perspective and a multiplicity of topics. Specific approaches-by-subject are of course tempting. Viewed in an autobiographic light, this fictional transposition of a criminal case covered by the *Gazette des Tribunaux* reveals Stendhal's father-hatred, his need for liberation from the constrictions symbolized by his home town, his particular compensation dreams, and his concept of seduction as a state of tension and hostility. From a psychological point of view, *Le Rouge et le Noir* provides a refined analysis of cerebral love—a delicate study of the early stages of passion—as well as ironic insights into the self-inflicted torments of an insecure but ambitious adolescent. Pride and timidity are at war in the psyche of this young plebeian, who is subjected but not resigned to the social and political pressures of his time.

The story of Julien Sorel thus presents itself, in part, as a social document. The climate of opportunism in the wake of the Revolution and the Empire, the attraction of talented young men to the increasingly centralized capital, the fluidity of social classes, the spread of bourgeois values —Stendhal diagnoses all these in his novel, often satirically. The worlds of Verrières, of the theological seminary in Besançon, of *ultra* society in Paris are presented in terms reminiscent of the most caustic pages in the *Courrier anglais*. The political and historical concern is all-pervasive in *Le Rouge et le Noir*, though it most often takes the form of caricature (The intellectual and spiritual divorce of different generations, the nefarious reactionary aims of a frightened Church and a devitalized nobility, the suffocating effect of a conformist and servile public, the very despotism of history—these are matters which Stendhal takes very seriously indeed) For beyond their immediate threat, these social and political factors raise moral questions: how is one to protect one's precious individuality? how is one to remain sincere in a world of hypocrisy? how can one use the weapons of one's enemies without submitting to their values? In other words (what are the possible strategies of self-defense in a social context that denies the priority of private values?)

Finally, *Le Rouge et le Noir* could be approached in terms of (literary history) as a self-conscious product of a writer exploiting a literary tradition, as a novel where Laclos' Valmont, Beaumarchais' Chérubin and Countess Almaviva, Rousseau's Saint-Preux, and Molière's Tartuffe all seem to meet, but whose combined and heterogeneous presence, far from inhibiting the author, allows him to elaborate, in devious ways, his personal myth of energy, spirituality, and freedom. (The novel raises the problem of literary realism, in particular the relationship between a given historical-social situation and its artistic reflection and elaboration.)

All these questions deserve closer investigation. Yet the topical approach when focused on a single theme or problem has its dangers—especially in the case of Stendhal. Few works indeed lend themselves as readily to misreading as *Le Rouge et le Noir*. Stendhal's taste for contrast and nuance, his technique of ironic disclaimers and inversion of values, the oscillating movements of his narration, his ellipses and understatements, but above all his habit of

STYLE

denigrating his hero at the very moment he enjoys him
most, and his subversive delight in thus becoming the
mouthpiece of a point of view he cannot possibly espouse
—all this makes for a fictional development that betrays
values in order to protect them better. Such an interplay
of meanings can easily disconcert even the most qual-
ified minds. Mérimée, who was not exactly a sentimental-
ist, blamed Stendhal for having revealed in Julien some
"atrocious" sides of human nature. Balzac complained of
the book's "sinister and cold philosophy," of Stendhal's
poignant mockeries, of his "demonic laughter." As for
T. S. Eliot, he felt that Stendhal was a master at debunking human illusion.

The tone and rhythm of *Le Rouge et le Noir* are more
immediately important than plot and character analysis.
Even a seemingly insignificant detail like the use of epi-
graphs at the beginning of chapters—a much exploited
convention at the time—can help the reader attune himself to the characteristic voice of Stendhal. For these epi-
graphs, at times completely invented (as the one attributed to Hobbes at the beginning of the book) are irrelevant
and yet deeply pertinent allusive devices that help establish a sense of intellectual complicity between the teasing
author and the alert reader. Similarly, the portraits, which
are often mere silhouettes, invite the reader to react and
collaborate in the process of creation. The first impression
of Madame de Rênal, conveyed by means of two hypothetical sentences, remains properly speculative: "This
naïve grace, with its innocence and vivacity, might have
recalled to the mind of a Parisian images of tender sensuality. If she had realized this type of success, Madame de
Rênal would have been quite ashamed of it." The allusive
and conditional method of presentation protects the very

intimacy it reveals.) The observation of a "real" character
by an imaginary one serves here to delicately nuance the
suggestion of eroticism, while stressing the authenticity of
Madame de Rênal's modesty. The *might have been* contributes to a fictional elaboration. Ellipsis prepares for
future actions and future self-discoveries. But the effec-
tiveness of such a portrait depends entirely on the reader's
rapidity of mind.

(Ellipsis) is indeed one of Stendhal's most characteristic
modes.) Sly, subversive, and intellectually flattering, it denounces a given reality at the same time as it camouflages
its own intentions. The building of a splendid church in
Verrières when Julien was a boy or the unjust sentences
of the Justice of the Peace, who is the father of a large
family, may appear to be gratuitous details. (I,5)* A page
later, we learn that the construction of the church and
the inequitable sentences suddenly enlighten Julien
("l'éclairèrent tout à coup"). A brisk stylistic pace corresponds to this sudden insight. There is danger that the
reader may not immediately make the necessary connec-
tion. Already the next idea—this is typical of Stendhal's
staccato of glimpses and suggestions—presses itself forward. Yet the church and the unethical sentences on the
one hand, and the illumination of Julien on the other, are
not only decisive in the adolescent's development and ambition but also symbolize the entire ethos of a reactionary
period, when the Church thirsts for worldly power, when
notions of individual dignity become dim, when the very
people whose vocation it is to stand up for justice are
cowed into servility.

To the ellipses of thought correspond ellipses in the ar-

* The numbers in parentheses refer to part (roman) and chapter
number (arabic) in *Le Rouge et le Noir*.

ellipsis: omission from sentence of words needed to complete construction or sense

ticulation of the narrative (Rapid shifts of point of view, calling for several layers of simultaneous interpretation,) almost totally abolish explicatory transitions. The following passage is typical:

"Monsieur Julien, restrain yourself, I beg of you. Remember that we all have our moments of anger," said Madame Derville rapidly.

Julien looked at her coldly with eyes expressing the most extreme contempt.

This look astonished Madame Derville, and it would have surprised her even more if she had guessed its real meaning; she would have read in it a vague hope of the most frightful vengeance. It is, no doubt, such moments of humiliation which have created men like Robespierre.

"Your Julien is quite violent; he frightens me," said Madame Derville to her friend, in a whisper. (I,9)

At first glance, hardly anything in this passage seems to interrupt the flow of the narration. The little "scene" begins and ends with a dialogue. But the author immediately draws us away from the interlocutress, and we see Julien from the outside, (objectively.) Soon again, the point of view shifts; by means of a conditional construction we are taken into the author's confidence. We learn what no outside observer, not even Julien himself, could possibly know. This is the moment when, having progressively invaded his fictional substance, Stendhal strikes. It is a swift blow. The sally on the revolutionary dynamics of humiliation has barely made its imprint, when we are again carried along. Already Mme Derville has continued speaking, or rather nothing seems to have happened except her speech. The Stendhalian commentary is submerged in the very movement which had drawn us to the author. The reader is plunged once again into the flux of the narrative development.[2]

Reading Stendhal is an exercise in agility. The capers and somersaults of irony, the juggling of contents, and inversions of meaning sustain a climate of ambiguity. Nothing can be more unsettling to the unprepared reader than the constant instability of the Stendhalian vocabulary, its shifts and reversals of signification. For "sot," "sottise," "ridicule," "faiblesse," are not derogatory terms at all when applied to the hero. They usually point to his charming clumsiness, to his inability to live up to his own calculating schemes, to his fundamental spontaneity. When Julien is "sot à mourir toute la journée," when he makes a shocking fool of himself with Madame de Rênal (I,14), we must understand that he is distressingly and delightfully timid in the author's eyes. His silliness is the very proof of his touching inexperience and emotional vulnerability. "He had a ludicrous idea in the evening . . ." (I,15) The "idée ridicule" is the announcement to Madame de Rênal that he will come to her room at ten o'clock that night. But the adjective "ridicule" is far from pejorative in context. Stendhal applauds his hero's awkward courage. In fact, the terms of blame, in the case of Julien, must almost automatically be translated to mean "lively," "natural," "authentic," "spontaneous," "endearing," "generous." Conversely, the conventional vocabulary of approbation must often be read as insincere and self-debunking compliments. Words such as "sang-froid" and "prudence" are simply damning. They are synonymous with "sec," "triste," "glacé"—in short, with everything that is stiff, frigid, and devitalized. This manipulation of meanings introduces a whole strategy of subversion into the novel, extending beyond the character of Julien to the social and political spheres. The reader learns to react and to think in a context where "no" often means "yes," where, in fact, "yes" can survive only because "no" is there to shield it. This fictional technique corresponds, within the rhetorical texture of the novel, to the larger issue of the protection of values. This precisely is one of the principal problems raised in *Le Rouge et le Noir*: how does one maintain one's freedom of spirit, how does one victoriously camouflage one's "heretical" views? Lip service to the infidel in power may be the only way to defend one's inner freedom.

(Ambiguity extends, of course, to all aspects of Julien's character, specifically to those that involve tensions between individual and social values. At every point, the author introduces elements that destroy the mental picture the reader might be forming.) This is particularly true of the early pages of the novel, where the hero's character begins to take shape. Julien's frenetic ambition seems to be summed up by his plebeian expression of horror at the thought of eating with the servants. "Je ne veux pas être domestique." (I,5) But no sooner has he made this proud and categorical statement than Stendhal informs us that this abhorrence of sharing meals with the servants was "not natural" to Julien, that it was bookish, that he in fact derived this repugnance from Rousseau's *Confessions*. Similarly, we learn in the same chapter of Julien's hypocritical visit to the church; but the very turn of phrase is tersely ambiguous. Julien considers that appearing in church for a quick prayer on his way to the Rênals' would be ("useful for his hypocrisy") ("utile à son hypocrisie"). But the need to perfect a role suggests that the role is not a congenital one.)(Only a fundamentally non-hypocritical person could thus decide, from the outside, to espouse the role of hypocrite, as though hypocrisy itself were a mask) The very nature of Julien's ambition is allied to lyric fervor rather than to materialistic calculations) On the one hand Stendhal informs us that Julien is determined to risk a thousand deaths rather than fail to make his fortune, but on the other, this impression of ruthless appetite for success is immediately corrected by the statement that success means getting out of his abhorred Verrières, where everything freezes his imagination. The notion of success turns out to be synonymous not with Machiavellian schemes, but with enthusiasm and dreams of escape. (These underlying suggestions of spontaneity and extreme sensibility, incompatibly blended with the superficial impressions of cold and ruthless ambition) are confirmed by two episodes. At a priest's dinner, to which the promising student of theology has been invited, he cannot refrain from praising Napoleon. (He immediately punishes himself for this grave lapse.) The second episode is more revealing: the tears he sheds and his crisis of overwhelming timidity ("invincible timidité") as he is about to enter the house of the mayor. Madame de Rênal's first impression of Julien is that he is a young girl in disguise. The impression echoes Cherubino's aria from *Nozze di Figaro* evoked in the epigraph at the beginning of the chapter. (I,6) Tears flow quite generously from Julien's fiery eyes. He weeps "with delight" when made aware of the paternal love of the abbé Chélan. At every point, Stendhal stresses the repressed and self-conscious candor of Julien's adolescent emotions.

(Conflict is at the heart of Stendhal's presentation,) and

it is of course at the heart of Julien's character. The tension is not merely between what Julien really is and what he would like to be; it involves dynamics that propel him to become what he is not and that lead to the discovery of what he becomes (and also remains) despite his self-imposed ambition. Timidity and resoluteness are constantly at war. The famous scene in the garden of Vergy, when Julien orders himself, in almost military style, to take Madame de Rênal's hand, describes the "awful battle raging between duty and timidity." (I,9) There is comedy here too, for Julien is so taken with himself and with his tactical problems that he fails to notice his victory: Madame de Rênal, who has to get up for a moment, spontaneously returns her hand to him. This blindness is almost more significant than the battle between intrepidity and timorousness. It prefigures other states of hypnotic surrender to violent emotions and *idées fixes*, as in the abbé Pirard's study or on his way back to Verrières to shoot Madame de Rênal. This blindness in the face of felicity—this inability to assess and possess the privileged moment—is one of the profound themes of the book. Only through the perspective of time past is Julien's happiness rescued from the obsessive contingencies of the present.

Other comic details stress this combination of timidity and blinding compulsions. On his way to Madame de Rênal's bedroom at 2 A.M., Julien is most unhappy to hear snoring coming from her husband's room. Now he has no excuse left for not carrying out his mission! But more ironical than his fear of success ("Rien cependant ne l'eût plus embarrassé que le succès"—I,15) is his inability to attribute his victory to the real cause. For it is Madame de Rênal's love, not his own clumsy tactics, that leads him to her intimacy. The ultimate irony of this passage is that concentration on his role as a new Valmont prevents him from enjoying himself in her arms. The puzzled question, "Have I played my part well?" thus logically corresponds to his momentary disenchantment with love and happiness: ". . . n'est-ce que ça?"

But there is also honesty in this struggle with one's self, in this refusal to take anything for granted. The scepticism is in large part self-directed. Julien not only imposes obligations but passes judgment and inflicts castigation on himself as well. After the emotional tirade about Napoleon at the priest's dinner, he binds his right arm over his breast (a symbolic pose) and carries it in this painful position for two entire months. What emerges early in the book is a morality of multiple standards, in which the only standard that really counts is the privately established one, imposed with arbitrary self-discipline. Such ascetic demands made upon the self, without the comfort of objective, external guidance other than historical myths and literary images, are clearly related to a steady self-depreciation, which is another form of blindness. Julien both needs and fears the judgment of an external conscience. He would love nothing better, we are told, than to find someone who could prove to him that he is simply a fool. (I,8) Yet he does everything to camouflage his real feelings and to disguise his acts. He thus has only himself to rely on for criticism and reprimands. But he is persistently wrong about his feelings and, above all, charmingly unaware of his real qualities. When he says silly things, which happens not infrequently, he despises himself thoroughly and even exaggerates the extent of his own absurdity. But he fails to see the only thing that counts: the expression of his eyes, which "were so beautiful and proclaimed so ardent a soul." In other words, his own spontaneity utterly escapes him. (I,7)

How to present characters who are self-conscious and yet totally spontaneous, that is the chief narrative problem for Stendhal. And it is in a sense his own personal problem: lucidity and enthusiasm, as Jean-Pierre Richard suggests, are the two poles of Stendhal's sensibility.[3] It would be easy to show how, throughout *Le Rouge et le Noir*, the protagonists' spontaneity is protected by their blindness to themselves. Madame de Rênal gives her husband a totally dishonest answer to conceal her pleasure at the hiring of Julien. But this instinctive impulse—the author explains —she certainly did not own to herself. (I,6) She gradually becomes coquettish, but—insists Stendhal—"sans intention directe." (I,8) Similarly, she falls in love without fully realizing it, becomes jealous without admitting it, and altogether fails to read her own heart accurately. Stendhal plays subtle variations on this counterpoint of impulsiveness and unawareness. The author's numerous interventions, often ironic and self-protective, thus assume a poetic function. The omniscience of the novelist protects the inner life of his protagonists, allowing them the necessary freedom to pursue their own dreams.

But the novelist's intrusions also establish a complex of tensions within the structure of the book. Disguising his enthusiasm through disclaimers and perfidious excuses, freeing himself from apparent commitment to his characters by means of disloyal asides, Stendhal exploits the resources of a protean irony for self-protective and camouflaging purposes. His characters' actions elicit from him patronizing advice, urbane maxims, discursive comments, and surprised exclamations. These interventions do not, however, arrest the imaginative development. Toying with the actualities of a given situation, the author constantly fabricates gratuitous hypothetic projections, thus creating fiction within fiction, as well as the illusion that the characters are free to chart their own courses.

This creative duplicity, so useful for the motifs of freedom, extends to the author's own temperament and vision. The game of intervention is often in the service of a cruel reenactment of his own past defeats, of a self-punishing exploration of his own poorly healed wounds. Julien's clumsy tactics hurt Stendhal more than Julien, but they also provide him with opportunities for self-compensation. The author stresses, and relives, the most vexing mortifications, at the same time as he grants himself imaginary victories. He contrives situations of embarrassment and frustration, but he also knows, and can hint at, what his hero cannot possibly guess: the proximity of victory. Only this promised land of bliss, glimpsed by the author, remains outside the reach of his hero.

The author's interventions not only guarantee the characters' lack of awareness of their success and of their qualities ("le vrai héros fait sa belle action sans se douter qu'elle est belle" [4]), but also give expression to Stendhal's fundamental *instability* vis-à-vis his own literary creation. Caught between the desire to move and yet not to uncover what moves him, he transfers his sensibility to his fictional creatures, and grants himself the privilege of reliving, but also of transcending, his private predicament. The real action of the novel is thus indistinguishably associated with the very process of writing the novel. It is a plot in which the author-subject, present to himself as though he were his own protagonist, has neither defined nor confined himself. His intrusive presence, his proclaimed lack of sol-

idarity with his own fictional creatures, paradoxically en-
sures not only their autonomy, but his own. This stance,
which allows for freedom, corresponds to the interplay of
past and present in Stendhal's autobiographic writings.

LEVELS OF TENSION

Although the very title of the novel suggests antithesis
(red or black, army or clergy, physical exploit or mental
energy, priest or hangman, fiery Jacobinism or somber reaction), too much emphasis should not be placed on its
symbolism. Color symbolism appealed to Stendhal. A few
years later, when he was writing *Lucien Leuwen,* he
again considered other color combinations as possible ti-
tles: *L'Amarante ou le Noir* or *Le Rouge et le Blanc.* The
title *Le Rouge et le Noir* was, moreover, an afterthought;
the idea of it came to Stendhal in May 1830, when the
novel was already at the printer's.

Yet the principle of contrasts holds. It is illustrated rhe-
torically, throughout the novel, by a mania for making
distinctions and comparisons. Julien cannot admire anything without first formulating a disparity. "Quelle
différence!" is one of his favorite phrases. "What a difference with what was fourteen months ago."—"What a
difference with what I have lost."—"What a difference
with Madame de Rênal's eyes." The refrain echoes
through Julien's interior monologues. It is as though he
needed these contrasts both to provoke and to justify his

most valued reactions. The habit of defining by means of such tensions can be traced back to Stendhal's own need to experience everything in terms of opposites. The world of Stendhal—whether that of Grenoble or of a fictional Verrières or Parma—is sharply divided into irreconcilable camps. His enthusiasm feeds on his capacity for scorn. Aversion and even contempt are for him propelling forces. Repugnance, for him and for his heroes, is the very condition of tenderness. Thus, in order to evoke lovingly the image of Madame de Rênal, Julien must first take stock of the coarseness and bad taste of Mme Valenod. The affective importance of contrasts is explicitly stated: "His distrustful nature made him rarely responsive to any memories save those which are evoked by contrasts, but such memories moved him to tears . . ." (I,22)

Love, more specifically, is served by the dynamics of contempt. It is her husband's "coarse laughter" that makes Madame de Rênal aware of Julien's "magnanimity" and of his beautiful, well-arched black eyebrows. (I,7) Admiration is here directly dependent on relief from distaste. It is around this very principle of opposites that the key scene in the library of the Hôtel de La Mole is built. When Mathilde de La Mole overhears the conversation between Julien and the abbé Pirard, she is struck by the contrast between the free spirit of Julien and the servile or "parvenu" mentality of Pirard. "This one was not born on his knees, she thought, like that old abbé. Heavens, how ugly he is!" (II,4) Her love—if that word adequately describes Mathilde's emotions—can perhaps be dated from that moment of illumination. Aversion and sympathy are locked in a permanent relationship.

No scene better illustrates this interrelationship, this function of disdain, than the ball at the Hôtel de Retz.

(II,8) The episode, largely experienced through the eyes of Mathilde, has at the center two "heroic" figures: Altamira, the Italian patriot who has been condemned to death, and Julien. But this admiring perspective is possible only because of the negative experience of boredom and general disdain. Mathilde haughtily surveys the platitude of good manners, the smugness of the "gilt-edged ninnies" who make up the bulk of her aristocratic relatives and friends. Stendhal stresses her mental yawns. But ennui, in the Stendhalian context, does not, as in the world of Flaubert or Baudelaire, imply an oppressive and ironically self-destructive paralysis of the will or even the yearning for nothingness. With Stendhal, ennui is eminently curable, indeed calls for a prompt remedy, and thus indirectly serves as a principle of enthusiasm. Boredom, much like execration, galvanizes the Stendhalian characters; it is almost the prime condition of fervor. This spirited potential of boredom is admirably summed up by the elliptic sentence: "Mathilde s'ennuyait en espoir." Symbolically, she makes a point of never looking at old men. She holds herself in reserve for the opportunity to admire. "Je veux voir un homme . . ." is her regal request.

This imperious nostalgia for enthusiasm does not feed solely on scorn for mediocrity. It is rendered more acute by the fear of being, in turn, held in contempt. Mathilde, who is disconcerted by Julien's almost insolent coldness, begins to attribute to him a fabulous origin. His haughtiness makes him appear "like a prince in disguise." (II,9) His beauty forces itself on her imagination in direct proportion to a growing sense of humiliation. "She had been despised by Julien, and she could not despise him." This mechanism of contempt remains a permanent reality; it is

related to the themes of self-consciousness and almost assumes the value of an irrefutable principle. "He despises
others; that is why I do not despise him." (II,12)

The primary tension is evidently internal. The awe-
some contempt is first of all self-contempt. It is characteristic that Julien overcomes his reluctance to climb to Mathilde's room (he thinks her invitation is part of a plot)
when he considers the lifelong self-accusation of cowardice with which he would have to live. "But if I refuse, I
am sure to despise myself afterwards." (II,15) The real
difficulty of living is cohabitation with one's own anxious
self-questioning and reproaches. Love itself becomes a
pretext for a study in strife and apprehension. As for jealousy, it provides the best illustration of that state of *"imagination renversée,"* which is, so to speak, the chronic condition of private suffering of the Stendhalian protagonists.
Stendhal even suggests that anger toward oneself, "colère
contre soi-même," precedes the clash with others. (II,20)
Ultimately, the tortured lover becomes the accomplice of
his torturer. The *imagination renversée* is in fact what
Stendhal describes in *De l'Amour* (Book II, Chapter 41)
as the profound unhappiness of seeing oneself inferior and
vulnerable—"voir *soi inférieur.*" But this vulnerability,
this "dégoût de soi-même" is also a principle of fecund
emotions and a mainspring for dramatic action. As a good
disciple of the Idéologues, Stendhal always sees passion as
a dynamic force.

Stendhal complicates tensions within the novel by repeatedly stressing a state of disseverance between the author's voice and those of his characters. Mathilde de La
Mole, who writes wild letters and yearns for heroic deeds,
is so unlike the typical "Parisian doll" that the author feels
compelled to apologize for this unlikely type, slyly com-

menting that a description of a character such as hers is
bound to be prejudicial, in more than one way, to the
"unfortunate author." (II,17,19) The author's lack of solidarity with his own fictional projections produces a double ambiguity: it conveys a devious admiration for such
characters, who are "happily very rare," but it also conveys
the underhanded critique of a society that criticizes a
character like Mathilde. The other type of disparity between author and protagonists, neater though no less complex as a functional value within the novel, includes all the
occasions when the author chooses to enter into open conflict with his own favorite creatures. Thus, when Julien expresses his admiration for the architectural style of the
Hôtel de La Mole, the author intervenes to observe dryly
that never had passion and beauty been so far removed
from each other. (II,1)

Stendhal is, however, at his crafty best in combining
these two modes of intervention: apparent lack of solidarity with his own affective mood and lack of solidarity with
his fictional projections are typically blended and transmuted into a positive poetic value. The conditional approach—at once critical, contingent, and conjectural—is
particularly conducive to inventive suspense. When Julien fails to see through Mathilde's malicious joy in tortur-
ing him, when he fails above all to come up with the
proper tactics, the author jumps onto the stage:

One sees that Julien was totally lacking in experience—he
had not even read any novels. Had he been slightly less awkward and cooly said to this young girl, whom he adored and
who made him the strangest avowals: "Admit that even
though I am less worthy than these gentlemen it is nonetheless me you love," she might have been happy at having her
mind thus read. At least Julien's success would have entirely

depended on the grace with which he expressed this idea and on the moment chosen for doing so. In any event, he would have emerged well, even advantageously, from a situation that was bound to appear monotonous to Mathilde.

"And you no longer love me, I who adore you!" said Julien to her one day, overcome with love and unhappiness. This was about the worst blunder he could have committed. (II, 18)

The discrepancy between what might or should have happened and what actually did happen provides the double opportunity and the double satisfaction of establishing the love of the woman as well as the innocence of the hero. Surely, during this scene of anguish and embarrassment, Stendhal takes sides with Julien. The affective bond is undeniable. The omniscient author, by means of the questioning and speculative mood, sets out to explore his own past in search of conjectural compensations. He teases his hero. But the teasing serves to evoke sufferings with which the author himself is only too familiar. The conditional construction stresses the gratuitousness of this suffering, its "pure" beauty. For it is Julien's very lack of talent as a cold-blooded seducer, in other words his authenticity despite himself, that Stendhal asks us, indirectly, to admire. The mixed pleasure of reliving his own timidity and awkwardness is here coupled with the joy of glorifying the wretchedness embodied by the character. The critique of the character thus goes hand in hand with a liberating self-critique—liberating, because the author remains free to dream beyond the contingencies of autobiography, even beyond the concatenation of his own plot. He affirms his independence vis-à-vis his reader, while granting his character—as he also grants himself—the freedom to pursue his own notion of victory. The autobiographic element itself, as it is metamorphosed into the texture of fiction, functions to bring out a temporal freedom) The narrative construct permits Stendhal to fuse the lived occurrence with an ulterior interpretation, which itself remains fluid.

These ironical dialectics between the author and his characters are further intensified by dramatic struggles between the protagonists, which are characteristically suggested in military terms. Martial imagery is indeed not confined to the mock-heroic tone reminiscent of Figaro's aria "Non più andrai" (Julien, after his first tryst with Madame de Rênal, is compared to a soldier returning from parade); nor is it limited to the conventional love-symbols of attack, defense, siege, and victory. It is of course amusing to watch the inexperienced Julien confront Madame de Rênal's jewels and dresses—these "terrible instruments of feminine artillery." (I,16) But the metaphor is significant. His readings in Napoleonic lore constantly transform the most uncontentious situation into a field of battle. This belligerent approach to reality, this notion that he must be up in arms in order not to lose his self-esteem, becomes most acute during his turbulent relations with Mathilde de La Mole, during this *commerce armé*, which forces Julien to ask himself every morning: "Will we be friends or enemies today?" (II,10)

Nothing, in fact, could be more appropriate than this imagery of belligerence. If Julien is an assiduous reader of Las Cases, Stendhal himself has read with care, and remembered, Laclos' *Les Liaisons dangereuses,* where amorous seduction is seen as a "corps à corps" combat and where military terms such as "défensive," "rencontre," "ruse," and "petite guerre" stud the letters of Valmont and the Marquise de Merteuil. Laclos no doubt encouraged Stendhal to view love as a struggle of wills well suited to bring out the themes of energy, pride, and ideological strategy. It could be argued, of course—this would be the Marxist interpretation—that the imagery of embattlement corresponds to the diagnosis of class warfare. Does Stendhal not write that Julien's fiery glance expresses the anger of a young man "en guerre avec toute la société"? (II,13) But such an interpretation would doubtless be a misreading, for Stendhal is clearly interested, as he himself explained to his friend Salvagnoli, in "renewing the entire dialogue of love," and he was particularly proud of his treatment of the tense and highly cerebral "amour de tête." [5]

Stendhal's great achievement is, in reality, not so much a renewal as a transposition. For he succeeded in translating into modern fiction certain elements of the Clorinda-Tancredi motif of Tasso's *Gerusalemme liberata*, which haunted him throughout his life. (The notion of a love-hate relationship and the image of an amorous combat had an unquestionable hold over his imagination.) In *Vie de Henry Brulard*, he recalls how the sight of the legs of his "cruel enemy" (his aunt Séraphie) filled him with desire, with what intense pleasure he imagined pressing "this implacable enemy" in his arms.[6] Conceivably, Stendhal here echoes half-consciously the nocturnal duel in Canto 12 of *Gerusalemme liberata*:

> *Tre volte il cavalier la donna stringe*
> *Con le robuste braccia; ed altrettante*
> *Da que' nodi tenaci ella si scinge,*
> *Nodi di fier nemico, e non d'amante.**

* *Three times the cavalier the maiden grasps / In his strong arms, and thrice the maiden too, / From their tenacious knots, herself unclasps, / Knots not of lover, but of savage foe.*

Jerusalem Delivered, John Kingston James (tr.) (London: Longman, Green, Longman, Roberts, and Green, 1865), II, 49.

The terminology, especially in Part II of *Le Rouge et le Noir,* leaves no doubt about the nature of the martial metaphor that presides over Julien's relationship with Mathilde. *"Aux armes!"* he exhorts himself while planning his nocturnal ascension to Mathilde's window. As he makes plans for "the battle which is preparing," he calculates the movements of the "enemy," and undertakes an operation of "military reconnaissance" himself. Later, there is talk of a "great battle," of victories, of semivictories, and defeats. It is fascinating indeed to follow the stages of his "Parisian" love affair with Mlle de La Mole. Alternating emotions of admiration, suspicion, contempt, desire and hate, mastery and humiliation are all part of a mechanism of action and reaction in which notions of offensive and defensive are essential movements of a psychological duel.

These tensions, which allow for no immobilization and no respite, activate at every point a sense of projection into the as yet unlived moment. Strangely, however—and this is one of Stendhal's subtlest achievements—restlessness and compulsiveness promote the freedom to dream. External pressures steadily maintain a contest between parallel levels of reality. The protagonists' need to find shelter from outer encroachments develops inner resources of revery and unconstraint. Often, characters involved in an apparently absorbing dialogue pursue an independent interior discourse. Even more successful is the suggestion of a poetic rift within the self. Coinciding but uncommunicating external events and juxtaposed but self-sufficient mental unfoldings emphasize the fundamental independence of both the unreached "other" person and the "self" whose gestures seem to belong to someone else.

One of the most arresting passages, indeed one of the

supreme moments in the novel, suggests this *dédouble-ment,* or splitting of the self. During a verbal exchange between Julien and Mathilde in the chapter entitled "Une Loge aux Bouffes" ("A Box at the Opera"—II,30), we hear Julien talk as he overhears himself talking, and he discovers that he sounds not only *strange* to the other but to himself as well. The passage brings out the most sophisticated and most moving qualities of Stendhal's art. The situation is viewed mostly through Julien's consciousness. By a twist of events, he gains the upper hand, and, as it is his turn to make Mathilde suffer, his pretended coldness and aloofness succeed. But her visible suffering almost melts his own determination to be strategically cruel. He barely has the courage to resist the desire to admit his love, for he knows that he will lose her as soon as he shows signs of weakness. He therefore continues talking and pretending, almost automatically, and in direct opposition to his true feelings, while his heart whispers other words to him:

"Ah," he said to himself, as he listened to the meaningless words which his mouth was articulating, as though to foreign sounds, "if I could only cover those pale cheeks with kisses without your feeling them."

This dreamlike sequence, conveying estrangement from one's outer self, focuses on an inner reality removed from the world of actual deeds. It is the dream that has become the vital principle. The very syntax moves from general revery to specific and intimate contact, as the impersonal "those cheeks" ("ces joues") gives way to the personal pronoun "tu." The wish obscures the lived act. But even the wish is for liberation from contingency. Stendhal here achieves a poetry of silence and of unrealization, which protects and perpetuates the ability to dream. His hero, caught in himself, is freed from the vanity of giving pleasure. What he seeks is not erotic victory, but pure sensation. Tension emancipates him from submission to *amour-propre*.

FREEDOM THROUGH TENSION

The theme of social hostility is closely related to Stendhal's psychological themes. In the long draft of the book review he sent to his Florentine friend Salvagnoli for publication in the *Antologia*, Stendhal stressed his desire to provide a description of the "France *morale*" of 1829. He was proud of his bold account of very "unlovable mores." But it is significant that what he himself considered the most remarkable section of the book, as "peinture de moeurs," was the episode in the theological seminary.[7] "*Very well* le séminaire," he jotted down approvingly in the margins of several passages as he reread that section of the novel. He was obviously pleased with his somber satire of a morally arid world of petty *arrivisme* and hypocrisy. Behind the oppressive walls of the Besançon seminary, mediocre and lazy sons of peasants, who prefer mumbling Latin words to plowing the earth, cultivate the art of hiding their uninspired greed and develop proficiency in contrite gestures. For here there exists even an art of eating a boiled egg in a holy manner. These rustic types have become a political force, or rather a political

tool, for the militant Church intent on maintaining counterrevolutionary pressures and on preparing for an even-
tual civil war. It is quite clear that in these pages Stendhal considers himself a political diagnostician; they
closely echo journalistic pieces in the *Courrier anglais* (I,
pp. 184–185; IV, pp. 88–89), which point out the military training of these future "curés de campagne," their
ignorance, their potential fanaticism, and their crass desire
for physical well-being.

But the seminary episode also has thematic relevance. It
is, after the relatively protected world of provincial
Verrières, a microcosm of what Stendhal believes society
is really like, a lesson in painful contact with a hostile
milieu. "He considered his three hundred and twenty-one
comrades as enemies." Julien's attitude is, however, not a
matter of choice. He is forced into the position of "outsider" by the pressures of animosity. "I see in you something which offends the vulgar," explains the Jansenist
abbé Pirard. The inevitable hatred of the "others" almost
appears like a fatality weighing down on the Stendhalian
hero. *"Difference engenders hatred,"* concludes Julien.
But the proposition could easily be inverted. Hostility
produces estrangement, but it forces the individual,
through separateness, into the discovery and affirmation of
his independent self.

It is easy to see how such a separateness can be simultaneously a source of suffering and a fecund principle of
pride and self-affirmation. Ultimately such tensions bring
out the best in Stendhal's characters. Pirard himself, at
first a terrifying figure of inhuman severity, achieves his
true greatness through isolation and persecution. A victim
of Jesuit plotting, he becomes a symbol of noble steadfast-
ness. In the margin of the very passage evoking his selfless

struggle against Marie Alacoque, the Jesuits, and his bishop, Stendhal jotted down a self-congratulatory *"very well."* Quite appropriately, it is Pirard who gives the clearest formulation to the Stendhalian law of the happy obstacle: "If a man has merit in your eyes, place an obstacle in the way of everything he desires, and of everything he undertakes. If the merit is real, he will surely manage to overcome or get around those obstacles." (I,29) Freedom is to be achieved through struggle with constraints; tensions can be creative and liberating.

The political themes confirm this principle of strength and resilience through resistance. Stendhal quipped that politics in a novel are like pistol shots interrupting a concert. If this is true, then the flow of Stendhalian music is constantly threatened—by remarks on class antagonisms, political discussions, observations on the Parisian nobility, echoes of recent political plots. At every point, but especially in Part II, Stendhal pulls the trigger of his metaphorical pistol. But the explosions halt nothing. On the contrary, they have a stimulating effect; they are essential to the drive of worldly ambition and to poetic dreams. In Stendhal's case, one might indeed speak of the poetry of politics. Social forces are seen as tyrannical; yet they fail to constrict the Stendhalian hero. Instead, they unleash an energy, which is in turn converted into fervor. Symbolically, the novel leads to the ultimate confrontation of Julien and the vengeful jurors who proclaim his guilt and ask for his death. But symbolically also, the trial provides a magnificent opportunity for fiery self-affirmation. In a dramatic speech to his "enemies," the jurors—a speech which, like a great theatrical performance, seems to arrest the movement of time—Julien asserts his independent spirit, and transforms a condemnation into a stoic suicide.

Inequity and death thus become instruments of freedom.

Far more subtle than the dramatic affirmation of independence, and almost in contradistinction to it, a camouflaged freedom is proposed as the only truly successful defense against the evil pressures of our time. In the face of anonymous tyranny (the plight of modern man), rebellious gestures are inefficacious. The first duty of the rebel is survival, if only the survival of the spirit of rebellion. Almost prophetically, Stendhal seems to have diagnosed the despotism of a totalitarian world and the dilemmas of the oppressed spirit that chooses to "agree" in order to be able to think differently. The problem, as modern intellectuals have found out the bitter way, is how to maintain a private conscience and heretical views under oppressive regimes. Controlled dissembling may not be the noblest or most heroic weapon, but its artful practice can be made to serve noble resistance and secret liberty.

It is in this light that one must approach the complex problem of hypocrisy central to *Le Rouge et le Noir*. The terms and concepts are indeed there at the beginning of the novel (the visit to the church is "useful for his hypocrisy"); they accompany Julien to Paris ("the center of intrigue and hypocrisy"—II,1); and continue to echo in his mind during his prison-meditation on death: "Talking alone to myself, and a few steps away from death, I am still playing the hypocrite . . . O you nineteenth century!" (II,44) Paradoxically, however, the notion of hypocrisy also has a positive value. When Julien thinks of his happiness as he is about to leave for Paris, the theater of great events and of greater deeds, he imagines specifically a world of crafty schemes and of polished Machiavellian hypocrites. (I,30) But the mental image is far from derogatory; cunning is here the very proof of energy and manly virtue. Similarly, Madame de Rênal admires Julien's talent for dissimulation. As for Mathilde, one might almost say that she takes his masterful falsehood as the clearest sign of his superiority. As she overhears a conversation in which Julien says not a word which is not a lie or a travesty of what he really believes, she is more than ever captivated by him: "What intelligence!" ("Quelle profondeur!"—II,28)

One could invoke the Tartuffe myth, to which there are not only echoes but direct allusions throughout the novel. In church, young Julien explains to his father, he sees only God. (I,5) To M. de Rênal, he points out that his holy vocation does not allow him to read as profane a poet as Horace. (I,6) When perplexed about the course of action he is to adopt after Mathilde invites him to her room, he quotes lines from Molière's play, and cautions himself that Tartuffe, too, was ruined by a woman. (II,13) And when Mathilde's pregnancy becomes known to the Marquis, who heaps execrations on the culprit, Julien's answer is supplied by a line from Le Tartuffe: "Je ne suis pas un ange . . ." ("I'm not an angel"—II,33)

The interest of the Tartuffe myth lies not merely in the obvious theme of hypocrisy; it proposes the image of a part played out within a part. Even more significant is the fact that we are dealing here with an inverted myth. In the eyes of the Liberals under the Restoration, Molière's play assumed a militant political value. The numerous editions of the play in these years, as well as the nature of these editions, testify to the fact that it constituted an oblique, subversive weapon against the reactionary Congrégation.[8] It is curious indeed that the very remarks concerning the military training of the antirevolutionary peasant seminarists in the Courrier anglais (I,

184–185) should appear in Stendhal's book review of Mortonval's *Le Tartufe moderne*. Quite clearly, the image of Tartuffe represents, in the Stendhalian context, an ambiguous symbol.

The themes of hypocrisy—one must indeed think in plural terms—encompass a hateful reality and ignoble means of fighting ignominy. The world as it is, whether in Verrières or in Paris, is filled with moral ugliness masquerading as honor. Counterfeit morality corrupts even the potentially pure, and the pressures of self-righteous public opinion choke individual values. The only way to resist victoriously is to use the infamous weapons of the enemy's hypocrisy, but to use them better. The artful, or artificial hypocrite thus has a double advantage: that of not really being a hypocrite, and that of outsmarting the evil forces that threaten his disguised spontaneity. Ultimately, the hypocrite's role becomes a means of fulfilling a moral duty and of acquiring dignity. What is at stake is the conservation of the unique qualities of the exceptional individual in the face of the immorality of conformist ethics. Freedom is thus forced to seek refuge in dissimulation.

THE DISCOVERIES OF FREEDOM

It is not surprising that the prison theme assumes a protective and purifying value. Freedom through confinement is a paradox related to freedom through camouflage. Stendhal was, throughout his life, haunted by images of for-

tresses and prison cells. The Castel Sant'Angelo and the
Spielberg cast their gloomy shadows across his works.
There exist political reasons, no doubt: the Revolution, the
Empire, the Restoration imposed their different forms of
arbitrary internment. The *prison d'état* became a key
symbol of modern political tyranny. Penitentiary claustration is thus viewed by Stendhal as a particularly dreadful
form of human degradation. In *Le Rouge et le Noir*, Julien's first contact with prison life is the humiliating experience of having irons put on his hands. But there is also a
contrary valorization; the feared prison becomes the happy
prison, symbolizing self-containment and spiritual self-
sufficiency. He experiences, much like Fabrice in *La
Chartreuse de Parme*, an unexpected at-homeness in jail.
At one point, he blames himself for being hypocritical in
his cell, as though there were somebody there to listen to
him. (II,44) The remark is appropriate only to the extent
that it suggests the solipsistic inner monologues of Stendhal's characters, who are always their own severest
judges. Characteristically, at the beginning of this chapter, Julien complains that the worst evil in prison is the
inability to close one's door. No reaction could more aptly
illustrate the deep delight of claustration. And no statement could be more expressive of the pride of claustration
than Julien's ironic threat to Mathilde that he will ex-
clude her from his prison: "Je cesse de te voir, je te fais
fermer ma prison . . ." (II,45)

The joyful prison is not only the locus of a happy isolation. Beyond the "amour de la solitude," Julien discovers a
deeply meaningful poetry of elevation and grandiose silence. In the Gothic Besançon tower he occupies a cell at
the top, and from there he enjoys, through a narrow space
between two walls, a magnificent vista ("une échappée de

vue superbe"). This relation between constriction and in-
finity is further heightened by the nocturnal silence disturbed only by the song of the osprey. (II,36) The strange
pleasure of the prison experience is not merely that of
luxurious liberation from daily contingencies—a freedom
from care, which brings about mastery of "l'art de jouir de
la vie" and which is symbolized by Julien's delight in
smoking superior Dutch cigars on top of the dungeon
tower. It is the joy of meaningful tranquillity. "His soul
was calm." (II,36) And with this serenity goes a deep
glance, an almost superhuman lucidity. "Julien felt strong
and resolute, like a man who sees to the very bottom of his
soul." (II,44)

The image of the prison cell as a privileged place of
insight and of spiritual serenity lends itself particularly to
meditation on death. From Pascal to Sartre and Camus,
French literature is rich in prison reveries on mortality. In
fact, Julien concludes that his destiny quite logically led
him to incarceration, since he was, according to the abbé
Blanès' prognostication, fated to "die dreaming." Death itself becomes a pretext for self-measurement. Thus, on one
occasion, Julien declares himself to be twenty degrees
below the level of death. (II,37) The high tension of this
tête-à-tête with imminent nothingness raises the Stendhalian habit of taking one's own moral temperature to a
tragic and even speculative level. Julien's soul at this point
is almost altogether exiled to the "realm of ideas." (II,40)

The exalted prison experience is such that Julien's happiest moments occur when he is transferred from his lofty
dungeon to a dank cell reserved for prisoners awaiting execution. It is in this seemingly unpropitious setting that
he lives his most intense moments of love with Madame
de Rênal. The four walls of the cell become the symbol of

his private world of revery, as well as of a pure and impossible love. If, at the same time, the prison imagery suggests necessary ties and inevitable separation, it is because Stendhal's imagination is repeatedly drawn to situations that stress the poetry of unrealization. Obstacles, in his fictional world, do not only propel, but also provide shelter against the snares and the corruption of erosive reality.

The prison liberation is multiple. Tired of heroic poses, freed from the compulsions of his own ambitious temperament, Julien can finally devote himself to the *present* situation; he is delivered from time. The stripping of false values allows him to relive the past, and to make of it a new present. "He could surrender himself completely to the memory of the happy days which he had once passed in Verrières or in Vergy." (II,39) Now the "others" no longer count; he is released from their exacting glance, returned to himself, truly emancipated. Out of time and fully in possession of his own being—that is the enviable position of the Stendhalian prisoner-hero. But such self-possession can be achieved only at the end of a road. In *La Chartreuse de Parme* also, the Farnese tower and the retirement in the charterhouse occur after the worldly excursions to Waterloo and to the court of Parma. Julien understands that all his life "had been but a long preparation for unhappiness." (II,36) But this unhappiness is turned into the most positive experience. "I no longer have anything to achieve on this earth," observes Julien in this chapter describing his arrival in jail. The expression is one of neither resignation nor sadness, but of an intuited and deeply longed-for transcendence. Immediately upon making this statement to himself, Julien falls into a deep slumber.

Ultimately, it is death itself that is the great reliever

from the oppression of time. The sight of the senile abbé Chélan fills Julien with inconsolable sadness and confirms him in his death-row vocation. As has been pointed out, Julien's speech to the jurors is not so much an act of defiance with political overtones, as a disguised form of suicide. That Stendhal's own imagination toyed with this notion is quite clear. M. de Frilair, the shrewd leader of the Besançon *Congrégation*, bluntly states that if the appeal is not won, his death "will be a kind of *suicide*." (II,46) And the Jansenist confessor attending Julien informs him that unless he takes every possible step to obtain his pardon he will fall into the "awful sin of suicide." (II,45) The suicide motif recurs indeed in a number of Stendhalian works. Octave takes poison, Mina de Vanghel shoots herself, the abbesse de Castro stabs herself; and it could easily be argued that Fabrice's almost ascetic disembodiment and death at the end of *La Chartreuse* is a particularly subtle form of self-elimination.

The typical patterns of Stendhal's imagination connect the themes of liberation with the themes of self-knowledge and self-revelation. The author pretends not to know his characters; they remain, so he claims, free to surprise him. The claim is neither a quip nor a sign of literary coquetry. The intrusive, digressive stance merely confirms that his personages are not meant to know themselves either—at least not at the outset. For Stendhal's heroes are not predetermined, despite the apparent necessity of a preexisting plot. They discover themselves existentially, through their reactions; and they even discover their reactions as a surprise.

Nothing is more revealing of this process of unconstrained discovery than the evolution of the love relationship between Julien and Madame de Rênal. When they first meet, the author makes a point of informing us that neither of them has read the novels which could trace out the part they are to play and give them a model to imitate. (I,7) In this respect they are the antithesis of Flaubert's protagonists who have heard, read, and learned too much, and who necessarily experience desire by proxy. The innocence of Stendhal's characters is no doubt relative, but it is effective. It is perfectly logical,—and thematically crucial—that they be blind to their own authenticity.

It is instructive, in this light, to compare Julien's first departure from Verrières with his second, and finally with the last meeting in jail. From suspicion to abandon, and then to full realization—that is the affective trajectory of the novel. When Julien takes leave of his mistress and enters the Besançon seminary, he completely misunderstands the meaning of her silence and frigidity. (I,23) She appears to him as a "barely animated corpse." Concerned only with his own pride, he fails to notice the convulsive and tragic nature of her reactions. It is only retrospectively, and characteristically too late, that he is deeply moved by the "cold embraces of this living corpse." The scene suggests, through powerful understatement, a bond between worldly and transcendental love, between the temporal and the eternal orders.

The second departure, which marks the end of Part I, takes place in a climate of passion and light-heartedness. The chapter comes very close to comedy, almost in a theatrical sense (there is an echo of Chérubin's window escape in *Le Mariage de Figaro*); yet these pages also penetrate new poetic and psychological depths. Madame de Rênal's sudden changes of mood, the range of her temperament, her "sudden gaiety" and impetuous movements of passion correspond to a revelation taking place in the

mind of Julien: "What a superior woman!" But the revelation implies far more than the delighted appreciation of
a lover. Julien has experienced this kind of revelation—almost somber in its intensity—earlier, during the sickness
of Madame de Rênal's young son, when he was able to
measure and to value the moral sacrifice made out of love
for him. (I,19) In the scene preceding his departure for
Paris, Julien intuits something more precious still than
this victory over morality and even religion (echoes of
Valmont's seduction of the Présidente de Tourvel). Hidden and locked up by Madame de Rênal in one of the
rooms of the house, he begins to see the beauty of uninhibited gestures and authentic responses. He is Madame de
Rênal's "prisonnier" when he has this revelation. (I,30)

It is in the real prison, however, within close range of
death, that the ultimate descent into the self takes place,
and Julien discovers the poetry of the privileged moment,
"l'art de jouir de la vie." (II,40) The atemporal delight in
pure experience or sensation is not unrelated to Rousseau,
and it is hardly surprising that Stendhal's clearest formulation of this mystique of the privileged moment in *Vie de
Henry Brulard* ("Pour un tel moment il vaut la peine
d'avoir vécu") occurs at the point of the most intense evocation of *La Nouvelle Héloïse*.[9] But it is the privileged
moment neither of an irretrievable past nor of a transitory
present. At no point does Julien prove himself guilty of
the sinful wish denounced by Goethe: "Verweile doch,
du bist so schön!" ("O do remain, you are so beautiful!")
Protected from smugness and decay, the Stendhalian hero
achieves his allegiance to happiness through a telescoping
of time. The retrospective event is brought into the present; but soon after, death prevents this retrospective joy
from degenerating into a commonplace satisfaction. There

is a deep poetic significance to the abrupt endings of Stendhal's two major novels.

The fundamental discovery is, of course, that of identity, which only the act of living and the experience of having lived can reveal. The twin themes of father-rejection and of father-search occupy the heart of *Le Rouge et le Noir*. The myth of a new paternity not only enhances Julien in his own eyes or in the eyes of those who admire or envy him, but is also bound up with the significance of his destiny and of his freedom. Mathilde imagines that he is a glamorous "disguised prince." Elsewhere, she toys with the idea that he is the "natural son" of a country squire. (II,9,12) But the notion is not merely the product of an amorous and romantic mind. Julien himself chooses to believe it, and so do those who cross his path. He considers the abbé Pirard, for instance, as a new father ("j'ai retrouvé un père en vous"), and the abbé in turn suspects that the favors of the Marquis de La Mole point to a prestigious though hidden origin. (II,1) More interesting still, the Marquis, suffering from gout, receives Julien's visits, wants him to wear a special blue suit he had made for him, and treats him as the "younger brother of the Count de Chaulnes, that is to say, the son of my friend the old Duke." (II,7) This make-believe is more than a game. The Marquis' desire to "ennoble" Julien parallels a latent dream that all of Stendhal's characters possess: the dream of a self-wrought nobility. When the dream appears realized, when Julien has been commissioned lieutenant of hussars with the dashing name of M. le chevalier Julien Sorel de La Vernaye, he can rightfully say: "I have come to the end of my romance" ("mon roman est fini"—II,34). There will of course be another ending, more tragic and more symbolically meaningful; but the basic revelation is clearly indicated by the first. The independently achieved identity is an answer to the filial anguish of the early chapters. "And I, too, am a kind of foundling . . ." (I,7), he murmurs to himself at a time when he already strives to take possession of himself. But in these early pages of the novel he does not yet know that self-possession and freedom can be achieved only through a surrender to happiness.

4

LUCIEN LEUWEN

the Dilemmas of Freedom

FIRST IMPRESSIONS

This massive, incompleted novel is possibly Stendhal's most ambitious project. In *Le Rouge et le Noir*, politics and contemporary history constitute the background to the hero's private destiny. Some years later, in *La Chartreuse de Parme*, Stendhal was to achieve an astonishing poetic stylization of political and historical reality. In *Lucien Leuwen*, he undertook a systematic survey. The moral climate under Louis-Philippe's constitutional monarchy, the new political role of the army, the power of the financial world, the mores and maneuvers of ministers and deputies, the tactics of electoral campaigns, the growing tensions of class consciousness—all these Stendhal combined with the love story of a banker's son, frustrated in his amorous enterprises, in quest of himself. Private concerns and collective issues meet at a dramatic crossroad. *Lucien Leuwen* is a text that no history of literary realism can afford to neglect, yet it is at best a fascinating failure.

It is not altogether fair, of course, to judge the novel as it stands. Only the first two of the projected three parts were written, or partially written. The idea of the last part, which was to describe diplomatic circles in Rome, was given up by Stendhal, although he had a few years earlier penned some interesting pages about a love affair with an ambassadress in *Une Position sociale* (1832). His consular duties in Civitavecchia were not, it would seem, propitious to writing. Although he was more convinced than ever of his vocation to "fill paper"—"empir le carte," as his beloved Ariosto put it—neither *Souvenirs d'égotisme,* nor *Vie de Henry Brulard,* nor *Lucien Leuwen* was completed. The manuscript of *Lucien Leuwen,* filled with overlappings, duplications, riddles, and gaps, imposes on the editor the impossible responsibility of deciphering, selecting, arranging, and establishing some continuity between the skeletal sections on the one hand and the clearly overwritten ones on the other. To further confuse the issue, the five volumes of the manuscript occasionally carry four different paginations.

The defects of the novel are obvious. Aside from its being now too sketchy and now too cluttered, the text is loose in construction and often lacks a clear focus. Satirical impulses tend to submerge the sentimental plot. Lengthy dialogues, especially in the second part, weigh down on the action and fail to live up to the author's witty intentions. Even worse, no apparent inner necessity propels either the protagonist or the external action. Artificially created hurdles, episodic figures, and digressions create a climate of diffusion and gratuitousness. Nowhere is Stendhal's narrative self-consciousness more acute. Nowhere does he appear in greater need of self-justification and self-consolation.

Yet the many tensions and frustrations of the novel also point to its human and literary qualities. *"I write upon the sensations of 1819,"* Stendhal jotted down in his peculiar English in the margin of the manuscript. These sensations, he added, were as fresh as those of yesterday, though fifteen years had elapsed. The allusion is clearly to the unhappy episode with Métilde Dembowski in Milan. Not that the novel grew out of a deliberate attempt to recapture the past; it was the activity of writing that resuscitated emotions. Involuntary memory was thus associated with the very process of creation. Stendhal himself was surprised by these echoes from the past, as testified to by his marginal scribblings and exclamations: "Ah, Dominique *himself!"* (Dominique is one of the pseudonyms of which he was fondest); or again, after the episode of the letters: "Et seize ans *after I write upon!"*[1] The entire first part of the novel is thus a happy encounter between the creative impulse and past affective states that the slightest provocation can bring back to life. But the provocation is never planned. The weakness, and also the strength, of the book is that the author, deprived of a preestablished plot line, literally does not quite know where he is going.

It is hardly surprising that the birth and growth of love should be evoked here with particular sharpness. In no other text does Stendhal stress so insistently the inhibiting *pudeur* of his heroine and the poetic appeal of her moral claustration. Nowhere is his unconscious search for retrospective compensation so clear. The feminine modesty of

Mme de Chasteller and the timid clumsiness of Lucien permit, at every point, hypothetical and speculative glimpses into *what might have been*. This creation of fiction within fiction, this exploitation of the misunderstandings and doubts during the early stages of love, this atmosphere of meaningful incommunicability, make *Lucien Leuwen* Stendhal's most searching love story. It is also his most vehement affirmation of anti-Don Juan values. At critical moments, Lucien is paralyzed by self-consciousness. The greater his awareness of Mme de Chasteller's beauty, the less his ability to act and to seduce. The lover's inefficiency is thus in direct proportion to his ability to be deeply moved. His "raisonnements admiratifs" go hand in hand with a ridiculous ineptitude. But Lucien's awkwardness, though it often makes a fool of him, constitutes his charm and ennobles him. The author cruelly explains that Lucien did not exaggerate his own ineptness, but he also, almost in the same breath, explains that the only person in whose eyes he does not want to appear foolish holds an altogether favorable opinion of his gaucherie (20).*

The secret, compensatory victory is, of course, visible only to the omniscient author's retrospective and re-creative glance and explains why he steadily glorifies his hero's naïveté and lack of proficiency. Nothing Lucien ever achieves is attributed to skill, and his inexperience guarantees the authenticity of his feelings. If ever he is adroit, it is not due to determination or talent, but to chance—"hasard tout pur." (28) This systematic and paradoxical debunking parallels the poetry of unawareness that characterizes Stendhal's fiction. For Lucien is almost chronically unable to assess his own situation and is blind to his vir-

* Numbers in parentheses refer to the chapter numbers in *Lucien Leuwen*, 3 vols. (Paris: Divan, 1929).

tues and victories. He thus fails to realize that Mme de Chasteller has changed her manner toward him quite early in the game. (14) After the ball, he is totally unable to notice the extent of his success. (19) Sitting in front of her window, he is entirely blind to the fact that she loves him madly at that very moment. (21) And of course he cannot know that she spends hours behind her shutters waiting for him to appear. (22) Similarly, he cannot evaluate the impact of his letters, never suspects that she would willingly allow herself to be kissed by him, and systematically misinterprets her anger, which is aimed not at him but at herself. Above all, Lucien never guesses how easy it would be to force Mme de Chasteller to admit her love for him. (32) The incredible ease with which he is duped by the wild stratagem of Docteur Du Poirier, who succeeds in making him believe that the woman he loves has just given birth to an illegitimate child, only confirms the mental climate of undiscernment.

Lucien's touching blindness, one of the meaningful themes in the novel, is part of a larger pattern of understated, lyric experience. As Lucien and Mme de Chasteller listen to Mozart in the rustic café, *Le Chasseur vert*, they experience one of those rare moments of Stendhalian felicity when everything contributes to a privileged and fleeting harmony. (23) The soft, slow music echoes the "touching obscurity of the deep woods." Stendhal slyly observes that an enchanting evening such as this may be counted among the greatest enemies of frigidity. The intimacy of the amorous echo is ironically attributed by Stendhal to music and poetic trees, when it is, in fact, the boon of unjaded sensibilities. The result is an epiphany of immaterial pleasure. "It is for such rare moments that it is worth living." The fragile and subdued lyric experience is directly linked to a state of innocence and non-lucidity. The passage, stressing depth and obscurity, appropriately ends with a musical silence:

Les cors bohèmes étaient délicieux à entendre dans le lointain. Il s'établit un profond silence. (26)

This silence is the symbol of a meaning that transcends words and perspicuity.

There are also non-lyric qualities that provide the usual counterpoint of satire and indignation. The arrival of Lucien's regiment in Nancy is the pretext for a biting diagnosis of social tensions and turpitude. The clash between factions, social groups, and political interests has its comic side, but points above all to a climate of suspicion and hatred. The worst symptom of this social pathology is the profanation and steady degeneration of values, symbolized by the low status of the once glorious army, which has become an internal police arm of the government. Lieutenant Colonel Filloteau, a hero at Austerlitz and Marengo, now accepts bribes and speaks of the need to repress political rebels ("réprimer les factieux"—2). The disease is, of course, not new; corruption and degeneration have been slow. "Happy the heroes who died before 1804!" writes Stendhal. (3)

The army, already discredited at the time Julien Sorel dreams of heroic deeds, is now a spy-ridden hotbed of secret agents. Delation is the least heinous activity (officers have received instructions not to read newspapers in public places). Far more depressing to Lucien than these professional informers is the shameful political role of the military, reduced to the function of a counterrevolutionary, antiproletarian tool of the *juste-milieu*. It is bad enough that a colonel suggests to a lieutenant the appropriateness of hanging an equestrian portrait of the bourgeois king Louis-Philippe over his commode. What makes it truly unpalatable to serve is that military service has become servitude—a servitude for the sake of a pernicious, totally unheroic tyranny. The cynical Docteur Du Poirier explains that the era of real wars is over, that from now on it will be the "guerre de tronçon de chou" against starving workers bold enough to protest their misery. (8) Rue de Transnonain, where a popular uprising was brutally crushed in 1834, has replaced the nobler battlefield of Marengo.

Lucien's regiment is in fact sent to the town of N—— where "seditious" workers have confederated and where a new version of military bravery may lead to a dishonored cross of the Legion of Honor. Lucien's sense of shame (he calls it "remords") is equalled only by his sense of pity at the sight of proletarian poverty and the squalid living conditions of the very people his unit is supposed to repress. The entire "campaign" ends with bitter irony, as the newspapers proclaim the glory of the regiment and the cowardice of the workers. (27)

A typically Stendhalian question presses itself to the forefront: given the moral situation of present-day society, how is one to be moral? How, in a world of counterfeit, is one to preserve one's dignity and affirm one's courage? The question is put concretely by Lucien, as he is sent on a dubious governmental mission: "If I am courageous, what matters the form of the danger?" (44) The scene of the election campaign is thus quite literally compared to a "battlefield." (52) In Nancy, Lucien seems caught between the ineffectual utopianism of the Republicans and the elegant, though selfish nostalgia of the aristocrats for a world that no longer exists. The dilemma symbolizes Stendhal's own dissatisfaction with these equally appealing and equally unworkable options. And it is characteristic that the moral issue should be put so clearly in historical terms: "Am I fated to spend my days between mad, selfish and polite legitimists who adore the past, and mad, generous and boring republicans who adore the future?" (11) Lucien's father opts for the world of the Ancien Régime. But that precisely is one of the major differences between father and son. Lucien sees no such choice. Neither nostalgia nor utopian dreams satisfy him. His acute, almost oversensitive awareness of the period does not permit him to escape out of time. He is committed to the *now* and yet is aware that he must strive to remain morally free. No other work of Stendhal poses the dilemma of freedom in sharper terms.

INSIGHTS

On the most obvious level—in fact quite explicitly—the manuscript of *Lucien Leuwen* tells a great deal about Stendhal's reactions to his own novel, his conscious intentions, his literary ideas and habits. No Stendhalian text is richer in self-criticism. Unlike *Le Rouge et le Noir*, *Lucien Leuwen* has come down to us in manuscript form. Five volumes, filled with the most precious marginal and interlinear comments and complete with dates and amusing sketches, cast light on the composition of the novel, as well as on the intellectual life of Henri Beyle during these consular years. Stendhal's corrections went hand in hand with the process of writing. Thanks to the devoted labors of Henry Debraye, Henri Rambaud, and Henri Martineau, many of these interesting comments are available to the general reader.[2]

These marginalia reveal the true nature of Stendhal's improvisation. Although *Lucien Leuwen* seems to have taken as a point of departure a manuscript-novel by Stendhal's friend Mme Jules Gaulthier, which she had asked him to read and comment on, Stendhal in fact worked without a developed original plan. He knew roughly what the sections of the novel would be about, but the specific causal necessity linking the sections and carrying the protagonist from action to action was missing. Stendhal was, moreover, as demonstrated by *Armance,* not a skillful constructor of plots. There is some bragging, but also much truth, in his statement to Balzac that the writing of outlines freezes and paralyzes him ("écrivant des plans je me glace"). The marginal comment in the manuscript of *Lucien Leuwen* is almost word for word the same: "Faire le plan d'avance me glace . . ."[3]

In fact, Stendhal seems handicapped without a pre-established plot line; this is clear from the text of *Lucien Leuwen,* as well as from the notes in the manuscript. He tries to justify a basic disorientation: "One never goes so far as when one does not know where one is going." But he cannot hide his concern. He repeatedly measures his enterprise against the "plan de *Tom Jones*" and frequently uses the word "outline." "This outline has the defect of always being a duet . . ." If one looks closer at the vague "outline," however, it becomes obvious that the author had excellent reasons for being concerned. "There, *I do*

not know how, he meets Mme de Chasteller . . ."—
"This, *or whatever I'll find at the end."* Stendhal is obliged
to admit to himself that he works best with a "ready-made
tale." [4]

Lucien Leuwen illustrates the special interplay between predetermined structure and "free" development in
Stendhal's novels. But this freedom of invention is not
only a difficult challenge, it is, to a large extent, an illusion. These developments seem free only because they do
not obey self-imposed patterns. A hiatus thus exists between the pivots of the novel and the substance that con-
nects them. Jean Prévost likens Stendhal's method to that
of the poet who links the few "perfect fragments" which
exist before the bulk is written and which, better than an
outline, activate the imagination.[5] Thus, like a lighthouse
dimly signaling from a distance, a draft of the novel's concluding paragraphs determines in an almost impercepti-
ble, yet deeply meaningful, manner the unfolding of the
entire book.

The exploitation of the "perfect fragment" is responsible for some of the finest pages of *La Chartreuse de
Parme.* The youthful army's arrival in Milan and the Battle of Waterloo had been "rehearsed" in other texts and
also in conversations many times before Stendhal wrote
that novel. It is because of fragments such as these that *La
Chartreuse* can move with such incredible speed from action to revery. In *Lucien Leuwen* the results may not be
so successful, but the tensions between plot and improvisation reveal a great deal about the typically Stendhalian
freedom to *reinvent* the self. For improvisation is here not
so much the attendant of invention as of rediscovery of the
self. Stendhal specifically denies any creative value to vol-
untary memory ("L'appel à la mémoire me glace . . ." [6]);

he prefers to take on a mood of affective availability and to wait for ideas surreptitiously, "en bon traître." In his marginal annotations, Stendhal more than once remarks that he is writing in a state of "dryness." But he does not tell himself that this dryness disappears only when the accidents of a narrative concatenation bring about a fusion of fictional impulses with spontaneous autobiographic reactions. Of *Lucien Leuwen* Stendhal might have said what he says shortly after in *Vie de Henry Brulard*: "I am making great discoveries about myself while writing . . ." (33)

Priority of the writing process over self-exhibitionism corresponds, on another level, to the priority of composition over planning. "Je fais le plan après avoir fait l'histoire . . ." [7] The proof that it is the spontaneous reaction that resuscitates the past can be found not only in the many observations pointing to an a posteriori model (as though the memory of that model came after the creation of the scene or character), but also in his surprise at the hovering presence of Métilde Dembowski behind every action and attitude of Mme de Chasteller. For Stendhal himself repeatedly marvels at echoes and similarities, which, independent of any conscious intention, carry him back to the Milanese episode—"*As at Belgioioso's place,*" he confides to the margin, opposite the passage describing Lucien's tremulous approach to Mme de Chasteller's house. But the reactions, spontaneous as they are, also imply a judgment of his past behavior. Thus Stendhal writes, facing the passage where Mme de Chasteller creates a mood of confidence: "With Métilde, Dominique spoke too much." Creation and self-appraisal are further related in the artistic doubts that resurgence of a private past provokes: "*For me.*—You are only a *naturalist:* you do not *choose* your models, but always take for *love* Métilde and Dominique." [8]

The self-searching impulse at work during the process of composition is rendered even more acute by a lingering awareness of a desired and yet intrusive reader whose imagined, invisible stare heightens Stendhal's self-consciousness. As he goes over the last few pages written, he records his concern: "While re-reading, I must always ask myself the double question: how does the hero see this? how does the reader?" Elsewhere he wonders whether he is sufficiently worried about the reader-oriented question: "What effect does this have?" ("Quel effet cela fait-il?") The critical and the self-critical anxiety are here inseparable. "For no other work did I feel so much modesty as for this one." [9] The marginalia thus represent a true inventory of literary scruples and assessments.

These provocative and sporadic self-questionings do not form a systematic meditation on the art of the novel. At no point does Stendhal anticipate Flaubert's conviction that there exist rigorous, almost scientific laws of prosody and construction applicable to the genre of fiction. In a letter to Balzac, thanking him for the unexpected article of dithyrambic praise on *La Chartreuse de Parme*, Stendhal states, braggingly in fact, his lack of interest in the esthetic laws of the novel: "Je n'avais jamais songé à *l'art* de faire un roman." [10] This is, of course, not strictly true; the swagger is invalidated by the marginal comments in the manuscript of *Lucien Leuwen*.

It is clear that Stendhal, as he proceeds to write, reads his own text with a critical eye. He compares it not only with his other major novels ("Not bad. The style is not too heavy; it is less uneven than *Le Rouge*"), but with the much admired *Tom Jones*. At the simplest level, his concerns are linguistic and technical. What has happened to the language of the upper classes in the nineteenth century? Is he right in utilizing the vocabulary of Mme de Sévigné, Voltaire, and Pascal? How can he be sure, being a thousand miles away from Paris, that his characters speak in a natural way? Has he not been absent from France too long to be able to capture the nuances with which language responds to a given political and social reality? He almost comes to the conclusion that writing a novel anywhere but in Paris is impossible for him.[11]

Another more specific question is raised: to what degree of abstraction should a good novel indulge? Repeatedly, Stendhal warns himself not to surrender to philosophizing; he catches himself in the act of writing like a "froid philosophe" who judges from a distance, too coolly and without sufficient sympathy for human foibles. The tone of La Bruyère (this "moraliste" influence on the French novel having been particularly strong) seems to him not merely incompatible with good fiction, but, in fact, a "degeneration." [12] According to Stendhal, the novel must *tell a story*, and it must do so in order to *move* the reader. Dissertations and ingenious remarks are especially harmful. Strange to say, Stendhal was afraid above all of lapsing into satire.

The apparently trite formula—"Le roman est un livre qui amuse en racontant"—has far-reaching consequences for Stendhal. If he insists in his marginal comments that the novel must appeal not to the mind ("rien qui fasse penser") but to emotion, he does so not only to ward off the satirical temptation, but to stress the affective experience, which the novel, as a genre, must communicate.[13] It is not by chance that he refers to effects "à la Raphaël" and "à la Corrège" that he admires in *La Princesse de*

Clèves and hopes to achieve in his own novel. Alluding to these painters and to lesser known artists such as Guercino is not idle name-dropping but relevant metaphor. It is in the same vein that he asserts to Balzac that many passages dealing with Duchess Sanseverina were "copied from Correggio." [14] Correspondences such as these between the arts, which Stendhal intuits and which later poetic practice exploits, clearly support the view that he abandoned an early allegiance to the "moraliste" and theatrical tradition (*Armance*) for the much freer experience of fiction as poetry.

IDENTITY AND EMANCIPATION

Self-criticism is, with Stendhal, more than a matter of literary self-consciousness; it corresponds to intense self-seeking. That is why *Vie de Henry Brulard* casts such an illuminating light on his novels. The motifs of identity and discovery, the elusive reality of the individual's becoming, permanently haunt his characters. Stendhal's worries as author are tightly linked to the obsessions of his fictional creations. The paternal bond in this parallel relationship between Stendhal and his characters is reenacted in *Lucien Leuwen* through the important presence of Lucien's father.

The riddle of the personality is heightened by the very fact that Lucien seems, at least at the beginning, so completely dependent on his father. M. Leuwen, who provides everything for his son (including a name-identity), thus stands as an obstacle to Lucien's self-discovery. And, paradoxically, it is the father who encourages his son to discover or affirm his freedom: "soyez libre, mon fils." (38) Yet, as his cousin Dévelroy (one of his external consciences) cruelly puts it, Lucien merely took the trouble to be born; his father continues to see to everything. "Your father supports you." (2) What would or could the young man do all alone? This generous father is an oppressive and repressive reality, a living reminder of the difficulty of being free: "What to become? To consume the acquired wealth of my father, to do nothing, to be good for nothing!" These anxious questions are raised as late as in Chapter 49. The stress is on the problematic "devenir" on which everything depends.

Becoming, in the Stendhalian context, has an unequivocal priority over being. When Stendhal, in his autobiographic writings, asks himself what manner of person he is, it is his actions and his mental behavior that he questions. Lucien's uncomfortable freedom takes, in the first place, the shape of a question mark. "Can I be answerable to myself for anything concerning myself?" (24) Lucien moves from surprise to surprise: he knows neither what he really thinks nor what he might think next. Self-doubting commentaries stud the novel: "I am sure of nothing concerning myself." (2) "I do not know what I want . . . What am I?" (6) "Do I myself know what I think?" (7) Love itself turns out to be a disturbing experience in unpredictability. "He understood nothing of all that had happened to him." (21) This poetry of astonishment and of inadequate conjecture is further stressed by the author's gratuitous intrusions pointing up the indeterminate status of Lucien's character: ". . . we do not

know what he will be one day." (21)—"Lucien's real
character had not yet appeared." (60) Even Lucien himself derives an almost spectator-like delight from his own
unforeseen reactions, although the titillation is unsettling.
When Mme de Chasteller observes that he is a strange
person, he agrees. "In truth, I do not know what I am, and
I would give a great deal to the person who could tell
me." The disturbance comes close indeed to fear—the fear
of not being able to account for the next moment. "I am
no longer my own master, I obey ideas that come suddenly
and which I cannot foresee one minute ahead of time."
(20) It is in this psychological context that the story of
Jérôme Ménuel, usually dismissed as a picaresque digres-
sion, takes on its significance; for Ménuel, to his great
surprise and distress, discovers that, among many other
things, he is also capable of being a coward. (8)

The themes of freedom are not presented as dramatically in *Lucien Leuwen* as they are in *Le Rouge et le Noir*
and in *La Chartreuse de Parme,* where the prison image is
a key metaphor. The prison motif in *Lucien Leuwen* is
less important, although there are some evident variations: the jail from which Ménuel escapes, the strict
monastery of La Trappe where Lucien dreams of seeking
refuge from worldly turpitude, the claustration of the
loved one, the cells of the state prison symbolizing tyranny. But although the image of internment is less central
to this work, the dialectics of freedom and nonfreedom are
developed with skill and considerable complexity. On the
simplest level, the problem is posed in social, or even sociological terms. The new monied classes seem to have
earned for themselves a hitherto unknown independence.
Docteur Du Poirier may be a caricature of the self-made
man ("I earned this fortune, not by taking the trouble to

be born . . ."—57), but M. Leuwen, the witty banker, is also an upstart, though an infinitely elegant one, who has acquired power and the freedom to do as he pleases through money. If Docteur Du Poirier, the vulgar parvenu, manipulates the provincial nobility, M. Leuwen can afford to speak almost as an equal to the king, even to intimidate him. Money is an obtrusive presence in the novel because it symbolizes a pervasive force and a growing form of pride. The humiliated minister Count de Vaize puts it succinctly: "A decree by the king creates a minister, but a decree cannot create a man such as M. Leuwen." (42) The extent of M. Leuwen's independence appears during the interview with the king, when he quite literally has no favor to ask.

But if money is a liberating force, it also brings about a new form of enslavement. Father and son are most clearly opposed on this point; it is not fortuitously that M. Leuwen's death is accompanied by bankruptcy. For Lucien, the banking business means fetters ("ma pensée devrait être constamment enchaînée . . ."—47), not because he fears the enclosure of an office ("cloué dans le comptoir . . .") but because he is repulsed by the vile *"métal."* (38) This aristocratic distaste for money corresponds to Stendhal's notion that concern for lucre exposes one to vulgarity, making true independence impossible. And is not Lucien's primary and ultimate quest the achievement of a valid privacy? Stendhal here diagnoses the inner contradictions of bourgeois mentality and morality. No other work of his so readily lends itself to a Marxist critique.

Similar tensions and ambiguities also affirm themselves in the realm of political thought. Lucien starts out by being summarily dismissed from the Ecole Polytechnique for having participated in some Republican demonstrations. Yet this same Lucien, who is revolted by the army police action against the workers and who in Nancy can truly sympathize only with the Republican Gauthier, also falls in love with the most unyielding *ultra* lady in town, fights a duel to prove that he is not a Republican, and sets out to conquer the aristocratic society in his garrison town. Once again, incompatible orders of freedom clash. While it is true that on the one hand Lucien's "amour de la liberté" remains a vital force, blending with his outrage at the sordid deals of a régime he despises, it is also true, on the other hand, that he is the beneficiary of the very régime he condemns, that he knows it, and feels guilty about being its accomplice.

To avoid facing his own inauthenticity, Lucien characteristically shifts the moral issue to the esthetic level. Liberty and democracy may be fine; but they lead to a reign of mediocrity. In the United States of America, Lucien feels, one must succumb to boredom and inelegance; there one must pay court even to the corner grocer! The Ancien Régime was corrupt and encouraged corruption, but at least conversation was bright. America, a symbol of reason and equity, is also a symbol of vulgarity and the cult of the dollar. "I would prefer a hundred times the elegant mores of a corrupt court," concludes Lucien. (6) By a twist in the argumentation, he thus establishes the priority of elegance ("civilization") over "liberty," because this liberty in a democracy is not of a spiritual or moral nature and implies the intolerable despotism of the newly rich. If the choice is between Talleyrand and the corner grocer, Lucien chooses sophistication rather than mercantile virtue. The implications of such a choice extend beyond the character of Lucien. Stendhal himself, in one of his interventions in the novel, ironically comments that liberty has unworthy lovers; in her magnanimity, she forgets all too often to ask those who come to her: *"D'où venez-vous?"* (57)

It is significant that Stendhal continued throughout his life to play out this political paradox. His middle-class heritage was constantly denied by his aristocratic tastes. He wanted and needed to see himself as a man of two centuries, of two cultures, and, at any rate, of two sets of values. The strange inversion of political and human values in *La Chartreuse de Parme,* where the so-called Liberals become the jailers, must be understood in this light. Stendhal sought to emancipate himself from an oppressive solidarity with his own social class by maintaining in his own life and thought a fundamental rift between political and esthetic orders. Neither an aristocrat nor a proletarian, Stendhal is the first of a long line of bourgeois writers attracted to the values they denounce, rebellious against their background, and, above all, aware of the bad conscience of their own social class. The political exploitation of symbols of liberty is particularly abhorrent to them. Thus Flaubert, in describing the sack of the Tuileries in *L'Education sentimentale,* ironically gives the allegorical pose of the Statue of Liberty to a slut.

Stendhal's notions of freedom must evidently be defined not in political terms, but in those of a self-protective disengagement from pressures. The difficulty is how to achieve immunity or obtain release. And the pressures of society and social behavior are the most difficult to elude. Affranchisement is here an altogether individual undertaking; no political régime can guarantee a meaningful moral freedom. Nor can any ethical system. Freedom must almost always be invented under the least auspicious circumstances. Can Lucien be free enough from

silly moralistic prejudice to be a full-fledged rascal—a real
"coquin"? That is the question M. Leuwen raises, as his
son is about to accept the test of government service. The
answer is implicit in the dual existence that Lucien proposes to lead while in the employ of the Minister of the
Interior. "I have sold myself body and soul to His Excel-
lency," he explains to the Count de Vaize, but this bar-
gain extends only to daylight working hours. "My evenings belong to me." (49) What is involved is a double
moral life. Such patterns of duplicity occur with regular-
ity throughout Stendhal's work. They explain the pre-
mium put on an intimacy of the happy few, for this
intimacy (this "parfum de sincérité parfaite"—62) is
permanently threatened by social pressures to which, in
order to survive, one must in part submit.

Love of pleasure and love of beauty are thus not frivolous indulgences; they are, so to speak, moral obligations.
Lucien's first glimpse of Mme de Chasteller suffices to
dispel all his "dark thoughts." (4) And these dark
thoughts, these "idées tristes," are focused precisely on the
oppressive realities of social tensions and hostilities. Love,
in the Stendhalian context, takes on a central importance,
not simply because it echoes personal memories and
dreams, but because it is the one area where private and
social realities come into the sharpest clash. It is certainly
not by sheer whim that Lucien's mind "crystallizes" for
the sequestered and politically reactionary Mme de Chasteller, just as it is not a coincidence that Julien Sorel se-
duces a woman of another social class, and that Fabrice
falls in love with the daughter of his political enemy.
Quite appropriately, Mme de Chasteller sits behind "her-
metically closed" shutters (5); her symbolic claustration

points simultaneously to feminine modesty and political prejudices. Symbolically, too, communication between the two lovers involves a permanent sense of distance.

But if Mme de Chasteller is the prisoner of her femininity and of her political opinions, Lucien is far from set free through the act of loving. Whereas Julien Sorel and Fabrice del Dongo achieve their most intense amorous fervor in prison, no literal prison of love exists in *Lucien Leuwen;* yet images of ensnarement and of entrapment in love occur repeatedly. Lucien, having discovered his own submission to Mme de Chasteller (his "slavery" to a political bigot), is compared to a "savage bird" caught in a net and set in a cage. (14) Similarly, the inaccessible lady herself feels uncomfortably subjected to another consciousness. Loss of independence, fear of an intruding and disruptive "other," awareness of a restrictive and fettering relationship—these are the accompanying symptoms of the phenomenon called love. Even M. Leuwen complains of the unhappy bonds, loss of independence, and loss of sleep inherent in love. "The first of duperies is to love," he explains, for once in an almost serious tone, to his son. (47)

Love and secrecy are intimately related in Stendhal's novels because silence and affective masquerade are the logical antidotes to this infringement on one's freedom. Hence Julien Sorel's dream to kiss Mathilde without her knowing it. The chief effort, defensive and on the whole inefficacious, is directed toward hiding one's vulnerability. "The main thing is that nobody notice my madness." (39) It is in this light that one should assess the meaning of Lucien's renting a furnished apartment ("Here I am free" —65) and of his toying with the idea of a false name, which only heightens the sense of emancipation. Stendhal does not hesitate to use the expression "the instinct of freedom."

It is clear that the themes of freedom in *Lucien Leuwen* have their most complex resonance at the psychological level. Lucien's very make-up remains perpetually fluid, as does the composition of the novel. Will he "gallop" toward the enemy or will he "run away"? (14) He does not know. There is no way of predicting. Nor is there a definitive manner of assessing what has occurred. "Have I acted well or badly?" (56) Again, he does not know. It is hardly surprising, then, that in a novel so concerned with the elusive problem of identity the father image predominates. Despite his encouragement, M. Leuwen represents indeed, as we have seen, a coercive force. The rental of the apartment is, in part at least, a gesture of rebellion against paternal encroachment. The assuming of a false name is an even more symbolic act. The father motif may well be the key to the entire novel. Though paternal figures recur in almost every novel of Stendhal, nowhere does the image of the father play such an important role as in *Lucien Leuwen*.

As Stendhal grew older he became fond of placing more experienced and cynical characters who know what life is about side by side with his youthful protagonists: Zanca in *Le Roman de Métilde,* Mosca in *La Chartreuse de Parme,* Docteur Sansfin in *Lamiel.* Through them he mocks and at the same time exalts the innocence of his heroes; through them he also punishes himself for his own inadequacies and for the hard fact of growing old. But these voices of experience and of bitter realism must not be confused with the figure of the progenitor, or his substitute, so constantly present in Stendhal's fiction.

The centrality of the father in *Lucien Leuwen* is attested to by the epigraph to Part I—a quotation attributed to Lord Byron, which Stendhal dedicates "To the happy few" and which extols the qualities of an exceptional *paterfamilias*. M. Leuwen, at first sight, seems an altogether different father from the vulgarian Sorel and the cowardly Marquis del Dongo. For once Stendhal grants his privileged hero the dream-father, witty, generous, and young in spirit, who treats his son like a peer. M. Leuwen repeatedly insists on preserving his son's freedom. "I in no way want to take advantage of my rights to *curtail* your freedom." (38) Yet the threat to his son's independence, the difficulties inherent in their relationship, and above all the anxieties of the identity-search and the identity-affirmation are brought out with particular acuteness in this novel precisely to the extent that M. Leuwen, the father, is not a villain.

For there is irony in Lucien's being called an "enfant content." (1) What this contentedness implies is an intolerable subjection. Though M. Leuwen wants his son to be happy, the happiness he conceives for him leaves Lucien little room for divergence of taste or opinion. It is only natural that Lucien is in a latent state of insurrection against this invasive affection. "I wish I did not have to rely at every moment on my father's resourcefulness." (49) The truth is that M. Leuwen—though perhaps largely unaware of it himself—wishes to manipulate not only financial and political affairs but his son as well, Lucien resents his father's desire to make his son happy "*à sa façon*." (65) And indeed, his father deprives him quite literally of even the briefest moment of liberty. If he is so determined "not to leave a quarter of an hour of solitude" to his son, it is because, as Lucien points out, he is determined to wage war against the "petits quarts d'heure de liberté" the young man needs to protect his own privacy and dignity. (43, 47) No wonder he ultimately rebels against what he himself, in an impatient outburst, calls the "sollicitude paternelle." (65)

Viewed in this light, the explosion is less shocking. It is not M. Leuwen specifically—he happens to be a warm and charming person—who is the target. Nor is Lucien a particularly ungrateful wretch. His remorse would redeem him. But the "grand remords" concerning his father is not so much for an act committed as for a state of feeling against which there is little recourse. "He [Lucien] felt no friendship for him [M. Leuwen]." (60) The "intimate shame" of not loving has little to do with the specific quality of these two human beings. Similarly, the deep "chasm" between them marks not merely the polarity of enthusiasm and irony so typical in Stendhal, but the need for and also the impossibility of a relationship closely enmeshed with the identity quest.

The father-son relationship is made even more uncomfortable by M. Leuwen's unavoidable role as judge. "*Studiate la matematica,*" he writes to Lucien in Nancy. (7) The painful allusion is to Jean-Jacques Rousseau's famous fiasco with the courtesan in Venice. Throughout the novel, the father and his substitutes, Coffe and Dévelroy, play the part of an external consciousness; and what they do have to say is hard for Lucien to take. Yet much as he would like to free himself, Lucien is bound to their judgment; he even yearns for it and constantly wishes to prove himself in their eyes ("Lucien tenait à prouver à son père et à Dévelroy . . ."—7); he hopes his father will have some "consideration" for him (9); he feels the need to "submit his mind to that of another and ask for advice." (20)

The reason is clear: though afraid of the intruding presence of "another" and jealous of his own autonomy, Lucien cannot, by himself, catch hold of himself. His own personality, by dint of his existential freedom, escapes him. He is not only incapable of assessing his course of action or of understanding his own character but also of observing himself accurately in the act of becoming. He therefore *needs* a judge and interpreter. "Good God! Whom could I consult?" (6) The most basic estimations elude him, "Did I act well or badly?"—"What opinion should I have of myself?" (56) And he is perpetually puzzled by his own reactions ("Do I myself know what I think?"—7). Lucien Leuwen is a hero in search of his character.

The novel thus marks the impasse of a type of *Bildungsroman* in which the hero's primary apprenticeship is not that of the world but of the self. Stendhal's refusal to indulge in aprioristic conceptualizations of a given psychology here causes, however, the absence of an "essential" stability and direction. This conceptual vacuity is in large part responsible for the particular failure of this novel; it may well have contributed largely to Stendhal's inability to complete it.

It is tempting, of course, to speculate why this novel, despite its good qualities, remains frustrating and why Stendhal gave it up. The consular life in Civitavecchia was certainly not inspiring for long-range enterprises. Also, the newly appointed consul's promise to himself not to publish anything while in government service must have taken some zest out of writing. It is revealing that all

of his literary efforts of that period—*Souvenirs d'égotisme, Une Position sociale, Lucien Leuwen, Vie de
Henry Brulard*—remain unfinished. Only back in Paris,
with Italy as far away as a distant mirage, was Stendhal
again able to write with fervor.

But there exist no doubt more serious reasons for the
failure of *Lucien Leuwen*. Gilbert Durand suggests that
a writer cannot with impunity compose a novel about failure and, in addition, challenge the imperatives of epic romance.[15] According to this view, Stendhal has here dis-
obeyed the law of a literary genre. Durand's somewhat
arbitrary premise is that all fiction follows a certain mythic
order and deals with archetypal contents. The heroic
themes supposedly always follow a progression from a
sense of destiny to the achievements of the hero and from
these to a fundamental revelation. *Lucien Leuwen*, inso-
far as it concerns itself with an unglorious period, suffers
from a "déficience héroïque" made worse by the inversion
and negation of mythic and epic patterns.

It is perhaps not necessary to indulge in such elaborate
theories. The secret of the novel's limitations may well be
more strictly related to Stendhal's specific problems, indeed, to the very qualities of his vision and of his themes.
Because he strove to create a character struggling toward
self-discovery and involved in the unresolvable contradictions of freedom, Stendhal was confronted with some
grave difficulties. A central character who, without any
objectively serious problems or obstacles, constantly creates seemingly gratuitous difficulties will no doubt tire the
reader and discourage the author. The subject was tempting, but the satisfactory tone and setting—the proper level
of tension—had not yet been found. At the time Stendhal
wrote about his rich young officer, he had not yet intuited

that such meaningful "innocence," in order to be dramatically valid, had to be transposed into another climate and set in a different key. The Italian myth was to provide him with the poetically dynamic and ironic unreality, as well as with the necessary elements for an allegory of escape. In that spiritual climate, Fabrice del Dongo, even more innocent than Lucien Leuwen, could seek and find himself.

5

CHRONIQUES ITALIENNES

the Exuberance of Freedom

THE MYTH OF ITALY

Stendhal's attraction to Italy bears all the superficial symptoms of escapism. In this respect, his case is not unique. Travel and geographic estrangement had, for the preceding generations, become a pretext for revery and the freedom to meditate. Though Stendhal contributed powerfully to making tourism fashionable, others before him had discovered the joys of strange places and strange mores. Local color and the literary exaltation of the picturesque were to become Romantic clichés.

What sets Stendhal apart is that his brand of exoticism is at the same time ironically lucid and emotionally profound. His love for Italy stems not from the search for surface titillation; it corresponds to a desired alienation. The words he wanted inscribed on his tomb—"Arrigo BEYLE Milanese"—might have chagrined some chauvinists but should not be attributed merely to lukewarm patriotism. A more significant psychological trait is revealed here. Stendhal's Italy embodies his need for a new and self-appointed fatherland and illustrates his quest for a self-created paternity. Projected into an ideal, private landscape, so to speak, this vision of a reality both topographic and cultural finds its origin and nourishment in a dream of personal freedom.

The same dream animates and explains many other apparently contradictory allegiances. A provincial who hates his province, a liberal nostalgic for the Ancien Régime, a critic of the Emperor who turns into his defender during the Restoration—Stendhal appears, at every point, protean in nature. This elusiveness cannot, however, be attributed to instability or caprice. Behind the contradictions, behind the multiform expressions, there is the steady pursuit of an authenticity that refuses to take itself for granted. His love for Italy was, among other things, a form of protest against the heritage he so despised. It is revealing that Stendhal attributes Italian ancestors to his mother's side, which clearly suggests the creation of a private mythology as well as a rejection of the "inferior" and unpoetic paternal line.

External factors do count, of course. The young Henri Beyle, about to be appointed second lieutenant, thanks to the protection of his relative Count Daru, had followed Bonaparte's army, which reconquered northern Italy in 1800. The crossing of the Saint Bernard Pass, the descent into the sunny and opulent Lombardy plain, the discovery of Cimarosa, the ecstatic first impressions of Milan, La

Scala and its way of life—all these experiences were to nourish, more than three decades later, the most poetic pages of *Vie de Henry Brulard* and *La Chartreuse de Parme*. The period extending from 1800 to 1802 marks not only Stendhal's military apprenticeship, with the unavoidable boredom and drudgery, but his first real emancipation from family surveillance. Italy was to provide, from that time on, a symbol of independence and individualism. But this early Italian experience—Stendhal was barely seventeen years old when he arrived in Milan—was also a lesson in loneliness and frustrated desire. All around him he saw more experienced and more enterprising comrades succeed with ladies of easy virtue. His own boldness, however, was confined to specialized houses where he was, moreover, unfortunate enough to contract a venereal disease that remained with him, as another type of memory, for the rest of his life.

When Stendhal returned to Milan in 1811, he was less of a novice. He became interested in painting, and his mistress, Angela Pietragrua, initiated him to the temperamental secrets of a "catin sublime," confirming his view of Italy as a country of great passions, jealousy, dreams of vengeance, acts of generosity and madness. From that point on, he had only one desire: to live in Italy. This dream became a reality when, after the fall of the Empire, he settled in Milan for a period of about seven years (1814–1821). He learned a great deal during this period: he studied art history, frequented the cosmopolitan society in Ludovico di Breme's box at La Scala, met Byron and Monti, discovered the *Edinburgh Review* and *Il Conciliatore,* involved himself in Romanticist polemics, and penetrated deeper into the currents and undercurrents of contemporary politics.

The Italian experience of course did not come to an end in 1821 when he was, as it were, expelled from Milan as politically undesirable. Many trips, many longer stays, and finally the tedious consular existence in forlorn Civitavecchia truly made of Stendhal the French writer of his time who knew and understood Italy best. The number of his texts directly inspired by his fondness for Italy is impressive: *Vies de Haydn, de Mozart et de Métastase* (the final portion of which is an account of Italian music and Italian mores), *Histoire de la peinture en Italie*, the several versions of *Rome, Naples et Florence*, the two uncompleted lives of Napoleon (the text written in 1836–1837 contains descriptions of the French army's arrival in Milan, which prefigure the opening section of *La Chartreuse de Parme*), *Vie de Rossini*, and the charming *Promenades dans Rome* (a cultural, social, and political guide to the Papal city). If one adds the more truly "creative" works, *Vie de Henry Brulard*, *Chroniques italiennes*, and *La Chartreuse* to this long list, it becomes evident that the Italian theme is of crucial importance to Stendhal.

The definitive study on Stendhal's Italy remains to be written. Such a book would ideally begin with an evocation of Stendhal's favorite landscapes; for Stendhal, so often accused of visual insensitivity, was throughout his life a sophisticated landscape lover. He compared the pleasures offered by a mountain or a line of trees to a musical experience. His privileged regions were, however, neither Tuscany nor Umbria; he preferred the combination of mountain, water, and vegetation in the area of the northern lakes. Next to the delight of walking in the late afternoon on the Corso in Milan, and of distinguishing in the distance Monte Viso, Monte Rosa, and the mountains of Bassano, Stendhal felt happiest near Lake Maggiore on the Borromean Islands, near Lake Como, or in La Brianza (now spoiled by factories) whose hills and melancholy cypress trees moved him. All these landscapes, transposed into verbal images or verbal exclamations, echo indeed like musical lines through his works.

But landscapes and climate interested him also because they determine and explain the character of a people and of a culture. In the wake of Montesquieu and other eighteenth-century relativists, Stendhal was convinced that the art, political institutions, and mores of a people are the product of a particular juncture of temperament, topography, and latitudinal situation. *Histoire de la peinture en Italie* contains some interesting developments on the specifically Italian temperament, which is defined as "bilieux," that is, vivacious, nervous, tense—above all, given to impetuous movements, violent sensations, and to a permanent sense of disquiet.[1]

Stendhal's acute historical imagination nourishes his private myth of Italy. He enjoys speculating on the specific factors that went into making the Renaissance, a period that fascinates him because he views it as one of the rare moments in history when man, uninhibited by social vanity, was most vigorously himself. Stendhal the atheist thus even appreciates and proclaims the dynamic role of religion. Were the Popes not themselves extraordinary men of action? Did they not set themselves above custom and law, and attempt to create worlds in their own image? Thus Stendhal takes particular delight in evoking the adventurous career of a man such as Alexander Farnese, who, after an agitated youth of *prepotenza* (insolent acts of power), abductions, imprisonment, and heroic escape, mounted the Papal throne, thanks to nepotism and the influence of a clever courtesan, and became known to posterity as Paul III.

In the outlined account of the origins of the Farnese fame it is easy to recognize one of the sources of *La Chartreuse de Parme.* The true role that religion plays in Stendhal's image of Italy is, however, more difficult to assess. One thing is sure: the man who said that God's only excuse is that he does not exist remained throughout his life an impenitent atheist. And yet his fictional writings, particularly his "Italian" stories, are filled with likable priests, nuns, and monks. Could it be that Stendhal forgave Italy even its religion? Or is one to doubt the authenticity of these characters' faith? Certainly neither one. Their religion is unquestioning to the point of superstition. And these stories are heavily loaded with details of corruption, graft, nepotism, and other more fatal sins.

The fact is that this apparent ambivalence contains a poetic and dramatic potential that Stendhal continually exploits. Religious superstition and worldly action are here interlocked as manifestations of the eternally rehearsed clash between destiny and free will. The simplest scheme of this dynamic relationship can be found in *Chroniques italiennes,* where religious inhibitions, often symbolized by convent walls, act as obstacles to love. But love and freedom most often win out. Walls are climbed and monasteries are raided.

The political struggles in Italy—those of the medieval factions, of Papal Rome, of the Renaissance condottieri— are also transmuted into Stendhalian motifs of audacity and freedom. Characteristically, Stendhal always associates his most exalted view of Napoleon with the Italian venture, blending it with his own first-hand knowledge of

Carbonaro ideals. This retrospective telescoping of the Napoleonic with the Italian myth finds its quintessential expression in the pages of his unfinished *Mémoires sur Napoléon,* which are given over to a description of Milan and of the French army's dynamic, "liberating" arrival in 1796.[2]

No wonder that Stendhal's discussions of Italian art are inextricably bound up with his notions of Italian political history and Italian love. The ideal book on Stendhal's Italy would no doubt devote some space to a discussion of his favorite artists—Correggio, Cimarosa, Canova, Rossini —but it would pay more detailed attention to the fictional utilization of Italian themes. For the Italian atmosphere grants access to the regions of Stendhal's most cherished values: the cult of energy, the improvised gesture, the generosity of passion, the ability to never forget. An austere sensuousness here guarantees the absence of the two vices Stendhal perhaps detested most: petty calculation and insipid frivolity.

It is characteristic that even Stendhal's notions of Romanticism should have a strong Italian flavor. The biographical reasons are evident. It was during his prolonged stay in Milan (1814–1821) that he was initiated into the Romanticist debate, which, in Italy, centered principally on the emancipation of the Italian language from the ultraconservative rules of the Crusca Academy. That there should have been strong liberal political undertones to these polemics is hardly surprising. Stendhal himself was eager to participate in this anti-Crusca battle. Echoes of these intentions can be detected in his pamphlet *Racine et Shakespeare,* to which was appended a text entitled "Des périls de la langue italienne."

Some of Stendhal's Romanticist ideas can be traced

back to the esthetic relativism of the abbé Du Bos whose *Réflexions critiques sur la poésie et la peinture* (1719) echoes the famous quarrel of the Ancients and the Moderns. But there is in Stendhal's pronouncements an urgent sense of the timely and of the immediate that goes far beyond the ideas of the abbé Du Bos, Lavater, or Cabanis. Stendhal believes that the artist creates for his time; contemporaneousness is thus not merely a reality but a commitment. As early as in *Histoire de la peinture en Italie,* Stendhal affirmed the necessary bond between esthetic ideals and sociopolitical contingencies. His chief Romanticist notions are logical consequences of this *engagé* view of the artist. "Courage is needed to be a romantic, for he has to take *risks.*" And this required boldness is of course in harmony with the specific taste of the nineteenth century, which, as far as Stendhal is concerned, shows itself avid for "strong emotions": "It is *passion itself* for which we are thirsty." [3] These ideas had already been expressed, almost word for word, in *Histoire de la peinture en Italie.*

Baudelaire, who was titillated by the provocative impertinences of Stendhal, adopted some of his formulas, in particular those concerning beauty as a "promise of happiness." Yet Baudelaire's metaphysics are miles away from the lyric hedonism of Stendhal, whose lack of affinities with the great Romantics (Hugo, Lamartine, Vigny, Musset) is a noteworthy feature of literary history. Chronological distance (Stendhal was their elder by almost a generation) was compounded with geographic distance. Even his theoretical predilections are colored by his transalpine myth. It was, after all, in Italy that he became acquainted with the *Edinburgh Review* and with the Romantic ideas this publication espoused.

Stendhal is obviously not the only writer to adopt, or even to construct, an Italy for his private poetical use. Italy became, indeed, one of the privileged settings for many Romantics, not only because of the surface potential of local color, but out of a deeper need for emancipation and escape. In the eighteenth century, it had been fashionable with archeologically minded travelers for whom its antiquities were symbols of time and change. The fact that Stendhal inherited this somewhat conventional poetry of history explains in part why, from the outset, he considered Italy an "occasion de sensations." [4] Literary echoes, often acknowledged, also sustain his Italian myth. Remembering his first crossing the Alps, Stendhal recaptures the specific association more than thirty years later: "I said to myself: I am in Italy, in the country of *Zulietta* whom J.-J. Rousseau met in Venice, and in Piedmont, in the country of Mme Bazile." [5] And indeed there is a pre-Beyliste quality to some pages of the *Confessions* that are colored by an almost spiritualized sensuality.

Nonetheless, Stendhal's image of Italy is his personal creation. In his early work, *Vies de Haydn, de Mozart et de Métastase,* he sees Italy as the fatherland of the specific beauty and the specific happiness that speaks to his heart and to his senses. *Histoire de la peinture en Italie,* behind the historical and plagiarist façade, further elaborates the myth. Italy is the country of love and of prolonged youth. "In this hot and idle country, one remains amorous until the age of fifty." The observation anticipates by some twenty-five years the recaptured adolescence of Count Mosca in *La Chartreuse de Parme.* But love, in the Beyliste context, is never just an easy surrender to voluptuous sensations; it is a fever accompanied by a "nuance de terreur" and by outbursts of energy. The blending of love and energy is, in Stendhal's view, uniquely Italian. And this energetic concept of love is, in turn, associated with the central Beyliste virtue of individualism.

In Chapter 131 of *Histoire de la peinture en Italie*, Stendhal explicitly refers to the "stronger passions" on Italy's soil, where "human vegetation" is more vigorous than anywhere else. Even crimes are admirable there; they reflect not turpitude, but courage and will. For this type of courage Stendhal conjures up a revealing image in *Rome, Naples et Florence:* "I love strength, but an ant can display as much of the kind of strength I love as an elephant." What counts is the maximum tension of will-power. Stendhal hates slackness. He prefers an enemy to a bore. The great virtue of Italy in his eyes is that its climate, its history, and the temperament of its inhabitants encourage fierce individualism. "Everybody dares to be himself." [6]

Travel has, moreover, a symbolic value in the Stendhalian context. Unlike Flaubert, in whose work exoticism implies impossible and self-destructive dreams, where movement is but an ironic form of immobility, Stendhal experiences images of geographic displacement as sources for self-discovery and liberation. Tourism is for him an assertive expression of freedom, for which an analogue in the very unpredictability of his style may be found. The meandering tone of the diarist, characterized by digressions, interruptions, irrelevancies, is nowhere better suited to the fundamental Stendhalian themes than in *Promenades dans Rome* (1829). Stendhal inherited the sense of ironic distance from favorite eighteen-century writers (Montesquieu in particular, but also Voltaire) who were fond of exploiting images of topographic estrangement in order to criticize obliquely the mores and institutions of

France. But the instrument of irony also offered itself to Stendhal as an instrument of delicate poetry. In *Rome, Naples et Florence en 1817*, he writes about Lake Como:

> The villages, situated halfway up the hill, reveal themselves at a distance by their steeples which rise above the trees. The sound of the bells, softened by distance and by the little waves of the lake, echoes in the suffering souls. How to describe this emotion? One must love the arts, one must love and be unhappy.[7]

This Rousseauistic description, with its underlying notion of synesthesia, which makes of Stendhal a forerunner of Baudelaire and Proust, is repeated in many contexts and in many registers throughout Stendhal's work.

THE ITALIAN "STORIES": *THE APPRENTICE-SHIP FOR LA CHARTREUSE*

In Stendhal's fictional writings, the exotic element appears first in what might be called Stendhal's "alimentary" short stories. These are not exactly hack writings, but they were clearly motivated by a need for money. The miscellaneous pieces collected by Henri Martineau under the promising title *Romans et Nouvelles* are, on the whole, not his best, though *Mina de Vanghel*, filled with reminiscences of Rousseau, and *Le Rose et le vert*, echoing his own *Lucien Leuwen*, are at their best fine fragments of novels. But the collection does contain some other pieces that are interesting for their foreign setting. As early as 1826, Stendhal published in the *Revue Britannique* a curious text, combining the story of the famous brigand Spatolino, the account of the kidnapping of the Pope, and a critique of the political situation in Italy. This early fictional venture—*Souvenirs d'un gentilhomme italien* precedes *Armance*—is really an anticipation of *Chroniques italiennes*. As for some other odd pieces (*Le Coffre et le revenant*, in the macabre vein; *Le Philtre*, a derivative melodramatic tale; *Le Juif*, an incompleted picaresque narrative moving through several countries), they all denote a certain submission to exotic fashions, but suggest that though Stendhal was tempted by the exotic note, he had not yet found his own style.

The catalyst for finding this style was the discovery, during his consulship in Civitavecchia, of long-winded, crime-studded chronicles—most of them dating back to the seventeenth century—which specialized in the detailed accounts of solemn and often gruesome capital punishments. Stendhal, who was proud of having braved the thick dust of Italian libraries for them, communicated his joyful discovery in letters to Sainte-Beuve and to his friend Di Fiori. It was clear that he intended, from the outset, to make literary capital out of this reservoir of violence. He had many of these stories copied and bound, and his collection ultimately rose to the impressive number of fourteen volumes. The consequences of the find were of the first importance. Although he published nothing for several years during the self-imposed "diplomatic" silence, these Italian chronicles nurtured his literary fever during his long leave in Paris (1836–1839) and played a crucial role in the genesis of his most luminous and most densely poetic work, *La Chartreuse de Parme*.

These stories, many of Roman origin, have been aptly called by Luigi Foscolo Benedetto a "museum of horrors." [8] This type of *storia romana*, often commissioned by some family and kept in its private collection, was usually given over to florid descriptions of trials and inquisitional tortures, of public executions, halfway between religious ceremony and grand spectacle for the masses. It is characteristic that Stendhal should have been drawn to these Renaissance texts, for he not only enjoyed the opportunity to translate and to adapt (giving free rein, as it were, to his "plagiarist" tendencies), but he had always been partial to sensational crimes. The *Gazette des Tribunaux*, to which he subscribed, provided him with the basic plot of *Le Rouge et le Noir*. And he was also an assiduous reader of *Causes célèbres, Chroniques du crime, Cour d'assises,* and *Palais de justice*.

It is not the trial and the punishment that interests Stendhal, but the passionate commitment implicit in the criminal deed, the élan that translates that crime into an eloquent expression of human dignity. Stendhal scorns venal crime. In the margin of some of the original chronicles, he registers his disapproval: "Common crime. Nothing new concerning the human heart"—or again: "Vile crime, family murder for money." His Preface to *Chroniques italiennes* makes the same point: "Crimes based on money are low; the reader will find few of them here." Nor is Stendhal interested in murder as one of the fine arts. What he understands by a "beautiful crime"—a "bel delitto"—is that specific manifestation of energy, the explosion of passion that transgresses the laws of prudence, transcends conformity, and at the same time reveals some deep truths about "le coeur humain presque à nu." [9]

The amateur criminologist, with his taste for dark plots

and vendettas, has in fact an aversion to cruelty. The very
names of Vittoria Accoramboni and Beatrice Cenci—the
heroines of two of the chronicles he adapted—evoke an
atmosphere of atrocity and even sadism. Vittoria is killed
while the assassin, twisting his dagger in the wound, asks
his agonizing victim whether he is reaching her heart.
Beatrice, during her interrogation, is tortured by being
suspended by her hair. Yet Stendhal is as repulsed by violence as he is by obscenity. In *Promenades dans Rome* he
expresses his revulsion at the "réalité atroce" of Pomaran-
cio's and Tempesta's scenes of martyrdom. Frescoes show-
ing a saint's head crushed between two millstones, with
his eyes driven out of their sockets, do not appeal to him.
Significantly, he reproaches his chroniclers for indulging
in lurid details. "The defect of this book is the quantity of
executions described," he notes in the margin. And again:
"Mere account of an execution." [10]

These Italian texts thus underwent important transfor-
mations at the hands of Stendhal. They were not merely
streamlined, but toned down and suffused with meaning
and themes that are totally absent from the originals. The
pamphlet *Origine delle grandezze della famiglia Farnese*
reveals Renaissance mores at their harshest. But even
Stendhal's earliest elaboration of these pages, which were
destined to inspire some of the key motifs of *La Chartreuse de Parme,* shows a poetic metamorphosis. The "las-
civious" courtesan Vanozza becomes an effervescent lady
(an "*aimable volcan* d'idées nouvelles et brillantes"), and
the kidnapping of a defenseless young woman by a lustful
future pope is translated into a sentimental escapade.[11]

Stendhal's *Cenci*, despite elements of incest, parricide, and sadistic carnality, is remarkably chaste if compared with Shelley's dramatic version. There is nothing

here of the old Cenci's "delight in sensual luxury"; we do not hear his victims' groans, we do not see the "wicked laughter round his eyes." Not only Shelley's terms and fascination with pollution, putrefaction, and "leprous stains" but the very climate of the play would have been distasteful to Stendhal. While the English Cenci-Satan proclaims that he does not feel like a human being,

> But like a fiend appointed to chastise
> The offences of some unremembered world

Stendhal's villainous hero is merely a *man* who wishes to "astonish his contemporaries." [12]

The happy blending of authentic texts and private mythic elaboration, of cliché and personal experience, led to the publication of at least four important stories, in addition to *La Chartreuse de Parme: Vittoria Accoramboni* (1837), *Les Cenci* (1837), *La Duchesse de Palliano* (1838), and *L'Abbesse de Castro* (1839). But several years before his discovery of the dust-covered chronicles, Stendhal had already written two texts that are proof of his long-standing interest in the Italian chronicle "genre" (*Vanina Vanini* and *San Francesco a Ripa*), and that suggest that this type of short story cannot be dismissed as a mere by-product of his interest in Italy.

In fact, some of the motifs dearest to Stendhal are embodied and developed in the *Chroniques*. To begin with, there is the peninsular myth. *San Francesco a Ripa*, which tells of a passionate Roman lady's vengeance against her frivolous French lover, perhaps illustrates this Italian image in the simplest and sharpest terms. Princess Campobasso, torn between the principles of her religion and the dictates of her passion, sacrifices her "eternal hap-

piness" to the imperatives of love. For this prototype of
Italian feminine temperament, love cannot possibly be reduced to a satisfaction of the senses; it involves her entire
being. Her French lover is somewhat frightened by the
"depth" of this Roman passion. But depth is not meant to
be an abstract notion. It is synonymous with intensity—
hence the juxtaposition of the expressions "profondeur"
and "âme à nu." [13] It is this very "nakedness" of the soul
and of the feelings that, in apparent contradiction to the
"hidden feelings of an Italian heart," is so dear to Stendhal. For it is, so to speak, an invisible nakedness, and
sums up his favorite paradox of a dissimulating and disin-
genuous spontaneity. This tension between impulsiveness
and that which checks and disguises it cannot be resolved,
but it confirms the preciousness of that which needs to be
protected. There is nothing shallow in Stendhal's "Italian" emotions. The "madness" of Princess Campobasso,
her "strange" resolutions, her acts of "démence," all convey the notion of a self-torturing energy that refuses to be
appeased.

Chroniques italiennes thus go to the heart of Stendhal's
fictional and autobiographic themes. Even the occasional
Voltairean note must not delude. The instruments of irony
and criticism contribute to an indirect glorification of
poetic values. If French vanity is derided, it is to stress the
beauty of unselfconscious commitment to overwhelming
drives. No story better illustrates, in all its complexity, this
correspondence between the Italian motifs and the deep-
est Stendhalian revery than L'Abbesse de Castro. Lovable
bandits, cloistered women, secret messages, dangerous
loves, total sacrifices point at first glance to melodramatic
and picturesque effects. Yet each of these picturesque and
melodramatic elements is integrated into the patterns of

Stendhal's imagination and into a network of meanings. The brigands, for instance, are not merely colorful folkloristic figures, but the embodiment of the opposition to the government (". . . ces brigands furent *l'opposition* contre les gouvernements atroces . . ." [14]), and as such represent the spirit of nonconformity and rebellion. Better still, they help dramatize the conflict between private and collective values, which only a man living after the French Revolution could so acutely perceive.

Ambiguity is at the core of Stendhal's writing, and is perhaps most neatly illustrated in *Chroniques italiennes*. Banditry, nepotism, and governmental corruption are the corollaries of personal vitality and a personal sense of honor that Stendhal feels have vanished from our bureaucratically efficient modern states. But beyond the conflict of standards of morality, which lead Stendhal to a dazzling ethical masquerade in *La Chartreuse,* there is the ambiguity of love and happiness. For love, in *L'Abbesse de Castro* as well as in the other "chroniques," remains beautifully unattainable, and all happiness is delicately tainted with tragic sadness. Thus Hélène Campireali, always close to the "greatest unhappiness," reads poems that sing of passionate loves feeding on great sacrifices, while Jules Branciforte diagnoses his love with a somber paradox: "Thus I can say that the sight of happiness has made me unhappy." [15]

The unattainability of love and happiness are clearly symbolized by recurrent images of love "at a distance." Jules watches Hélène's window from afar (so do the lovers in the Bianca Capello episode in *Histoire de la peinture en Italie,* and so do Lucien Leuwen and Fabrice del Dongo). Distant signals, secret communications through glances or coded messages—these are the favorite modes

of amorous approach in the world of Stendhal. One finds
here no promiscuity, real or imagined, such as one finds in
the novels of Flaubert, for instance. None of Stendhal's
heroines ever experiences the torpor and dizziness of
Emma Bovary at the Vaubyessard ball. None of his heroes
is ever exposed to a display of vulgar carnality as is
Frédéric Moreau at the Maréchale's ball in *L'Education
sentimentale*. The very claustration of the desired woman
is symbolic of inaccessibility. Convent images provide an
almost metaphoric texture. Hélène is first threatened with
forced reclusion in a cloister. Later, when she is actually
locked up in the Convent of the Visitation and Jules or-
ganizes an expedition to see her, the "dark walls" bring to
his mind the image of a fortress. This image is later confirmed and developed in the scene of forceful penetration
into the convent: the servants of the convent are, for the
most part, former soldiers; they live in a type of army bar-
rack ("caserne") with grilled windows; the walls are over
eighty feet high; and the interior gate is guarded by the so-
called "tower nun"—the "soeur tourière." [16] The entire architectural complex is forbidding.

The very immurement of the desired woman and the
walls that either separate the lovers or lock them up in an
impossible relationship symbolize the dialectics of freedom. Cells and walls imply seclusion, constraint, a kind of
death-in-life, but they can also—and often simultaneously
—suggest the protection of an inner life, the freedom to
dream, spiritual liberation. In the world of Stendhal, love
is never a smug experience; it is never limited to the sheer
titillation of the senses. It signifies a total involvement and
a dynamic projection into the very act of living. Love constantly marks a going beyond the imperfections of the
flesh and of daily existence. It is, in fact, almost a chal-

lenge to life. That is why the amorous plot so often assumes the patterns of an escape allegory. Yet, paradoxically, this very freedom-in-love is conceived within the context of prison imagery. This is the central paradox that Stendhal develops with masterful variations in *La Chartreuse de Parme*.

6

LA CHARTREUSE DE PARME

the Poetry of Freedom

A MENTAL LANDSCAPE

The words "La Chartreuse de Parme" suffice to conjure up, in the mind of a Stendhalian reader, a recognizable landscape and a specific rhythm. They evoke a fantasy charterhouse, which is not actually mentioned until the very last pages of the book, but is present in the reader's mind from the very beginning, as if to warn him that beyond the scene of political intrigue, savoir-vivre, and cynicism, there exists a privileged and almost inaccessible region: the world of hidden spirituality, the precious world of prison, retirement, and renunciation.

An impressionistic critic might stress the autumnal light of *La Chartreuse*. Distant details are repeatedly brought out in their sharpest outline. Yet this light, allowing for clarity and vast panoramas, does not provide a gay illumination. It has the softness of mellow sadness and resignation. It is a light that somehow suggests the eternity of the fleeting moment.

The opening section of the novel is a dithyramb to youth and impetuous unconcern. The momentum of Bonaparte's soldiers, who are all under twenty-five years of age, the explicit contempt for all that is old and bewigged, the contrast between the zest of this young army and the decrepit "vieux généraux imbéciles"—all suggests an atmosphere of inebriation and abandon totally devoid of any regret, devoid even of a sense of the past. Thus the grouchy Marquis del Dongo, whose reactionary fears make him hate all gaiety, and his young sister Gina, who laughs uncontrollably at the sight of her powdered suitor, belong to different generations; between them there exists, so to speak, a breach of moral and historical continuity. It would seem that even history no longer had any contact with itself.

Timelessness and the imperatives of time—these are indeed the conflicting experiences within the novel. The very structure of the first chapter conveys a scheme of action and reaction. It evokes a new era of happiness, which historic events interrupt and abolish. The French army, which liberates Milan and thus inaugurates a period of happy "freedom," is soon again defeated. Laughter is again replaced by morose and unenlightened ideas. But the happy period, precisely because it has vanished, proves to be even more meaningful in retrospect. The interlude colors the events that follow. The entire novel is conceived under the sign of lost youth, which memory and fervor reconquer.

The character who most dramatically embodies this theme of reclaimed youth is Count Mosca. This elegant, middle-aged statesman, who has known the exhilaration of the Napoleonic campaigns but who now submits realistically and ironically to the sordid game of post-Napoleonic politics, retrieves the ardor of his early years through love. As he waits two full hours for Countess Pietranera to appear at La Scala, he comes to the conclusion that old age is really nothing but the inability to surrender to delightful, adolescent emotions. These "enfantillages délicieux" are fully savored by the hedonistic Mosca. He postpones the moment of presenting himself in Gina's box and appreciates his own unexpected timidity. "Such a thing has not happened to me in twenty-five years." (6)* As much as Gina's charm, Mosca admires in himself this process of rejuvenation for which she is responsible.

The ambiguous tone of *La Chartreuse,* which transmutes playfulness into meaning and deals with the most serious events in an almost flippant manner, can easily unsettle the reader. This tone is hard to describe. Unconstrained and irreverent, it seeks out the sophisticated reader, willing and able to follow the author in his mental games and ironic capers. Stendhal's picaresque rhythm and humor are heightened by his mastery of understatement and ellipsis. False conjunctions, misleading parallels, inversions of meaning, and subversive juxtapositions are here used to support themes that the reader must learn to decipher. This allusive technique is essentially that of the conversationalist who seeks to transform his interlocutor into an accomplice. Lively and resilient, Stendhal's voice acts out a game of improvisation. At every point, though

* Numbers in parentheses refer to chapter numbers in *La Chartreuse de Parme.*

carried by the momentum of his story, he pretends not to know what the next episode will reveal. His feigned surprises, his self-induced reactions, stress the freedom of his protagonists. In fact, no novel is more steadily propelled by an inner, almost dreamlike necessity.

Irony and narrative distance are thus the masks for lyric commitment. Stendhal's smile, tender or sarcastic, must not mislead; no writer has used his own wit better to disguise and protect his own affectivity. Irony avenges Stendhal of servitudes to which he is only too happy to submit. The apparent gaiety and carefree tone prove ultimately to be as melancholic as the autumnal light that falls on the marvellous and oppressive Farnese tower.[1]

Landscapes in *La Chartreuse* are the concrete figurations of Stendhal's lyricism. Ever since his adolescence, Stendhal was tempted by the emotional correspondences between external scenery and private dreams. To reveal the specific affective resonance of the Borromean Islands had been one of his earliest literary ambitions. The "unique" position of the Dongo castle near Grianta, the view of the "sublime lake," the "admirable forms" of the hills, the secret language of these "ravishing places" in *La Chartreuse* (2) cannot be dismissed as a yielding to literary fashion. An authentic delight abounds in the Stendhalian evocations: the Lombardy plain, the Parma citadel, the tower of the abbé Blanès—real or imaginary places all of which suggest an Italy that Stendhal, for his own private use, transfigured into a world of revery and energy. As epigraph for *La Chartreuse*, he chose Ariosto's famous lines:

for Commentary

> *Gia mi fur dolci inviti a empir le carte*
> *I luoghi ameni.*

These *luoghi ameni*—these magic spots of Stendhal's mental topography—conjure up a world of spiritual inebriation in which the very senses are subservient to a delicate poetry.

The privileged place and the privileged moment represent a rare and fleeting conjunction. To attain and remember them justifies all the rest. Stendhal, like Rousseau, develops a cult of those ineffable hours that allow man to forget his contingency and to glimpse the real life of things, moments of grace when suddenly the voice of the world is still. But the privileged temporal and spatial realities in *La Chartreuse* also provide a liberating force. All the eccentricities, all the unforeseeable acts of his non-conventional characters, share the immunity of an enchanted transalpine fairyland—but a fairyland for adults only.

A climate of passion and of madness, disconcerting to literal-minded readers, reigns in this fantasy Italy. Enrico Panzacchi thus protests against the distorted vision of a country peopled with heroic bandits, histrionic priests, and poetic servants composing sonnets.[2] Stendhal's favorite characters in *La Chartreuse* are indeed capable of the most extravagant actions, as though the Italian setting itself inspired extraordinary deeds. Fabrice del Dongo, naïve and superstitious, runs away from home to fight for Napoleon at Waterloo. His aunt, Gina Pietranera, who becomes Duchess Sanseverina, is a woman who scorns prudence and adores her nephew, who kills for his sake and would do "a thousand times worse," according to the author. Count Mosca, a Beyliste Metternich, discovers not only the rejuvenating "folies amoureuses," but the furor of jealousy, which leads him to the brink of crime. Clélia Conti, whose face seems saddened by the permanent regret of an absent chimera, betrays her jailer-father and, under the most unlikely circumstances, saves the beloved prisoner. Capable of the most attractive crimes, endowed with the most unusual virtues, the Stendhalian heroes know how to despise with passion. Duchess Sanseverina relishes the joys of a shrewdly prepared and slowly savored vengeance. But this capacity to hate also allows the noblest Stendhalian protagonists to experience the raptures of a love so absolute that it ultimately induces them to prefer imprisonment, the refusal of happiness, and even death, to a worse undoing—a life that would erode their capacity to love.

It is this counterpoint of extroverted brio and tender inner music that carries the significant themes of the novel. *La Chartreuse,* like the opera buffa that Stendhal so loved, juxtaposes staccato recitatives and fugitive lyric moments. Prosaic and poetic elements support each other. Illusion and disenchantment, idealism and cynicism, negation and affirmation of values, parody and belief, aloofness and involvement—all these apparent contraries are tightly interlocked. The very unity of *La Chartreuse* rests heavily on its ambiguous nature. Even the last sentence of the book can be interpreted as simultaneously ironic and nostalgic. The order it describes is both the political order that denies life and a spiritual reality that totally transcends the derisive realm of politics.

Ambiguities

The most striking illustration of Stendhalian ambiguities in *La Chartreuse* is the famous Waterloo episode. Stendhal has been praised for his "realistic" account, for having been the first writer to systematically describe a battle from the point of view of a single consciousness, through the eyes of a single character utterly puzzled by what goes on, and who, instead of dominating the historic event with the perspective and omniscience of a historian, is only able to witness movement and confusion. Stendhal himself, after the Battle of Bautzen (probably the only battle he saw, and at some range at that), remembered that he had glimpsed all there is to be seen of a battle— that is, little, or nothing. With Fabrice at Waterloo, we are far indeed from the Homeric or Virgilian epic slaughters where every participant, weapon, skirmish, and wound is catalogued and described by the poet-strategist.

But if the epic description is debunked by implication, so is the epic hero. Fabrice, in love with the sound of cannons, thirsts for noble sensations. A romantic Candide, he would like to gallop after every one of Napoleon's marshals. He is, in fact, a heroic parasite, inexperienced and totally superfluous on the field of battle. The author treats him with deliberate irony. "We must confess that our hero was quite unheroic at that moment." Comments such as these stud the pages of the Waterloo episode. We are invited to laugh at Fabrice's naïveté, his clumsiness, his illusions, and at the deflation of his dreams of heroic comradeship. He discovers that war resembles neither Ariosto's poem nor the proclamations of the Emperor. As the author leads Fabrice from surprise to surprise, from blunder to blunder, from one humiliating experience to another, it becomes quite evident that what these pages propose is not at all a "realistic" account, but a mock-heroic episode, a parody of epic attitudes and conventions.

Conventional epic elements are in fact repeatedly stressed, but in order, it would seem, to attract attention to obvious discrepancies. A grand spectacle, a hero traveling far from his home country and involved in a series of actions filled with obstacles and dangers, enormous crowds, mysterious omens and predictions, battles pitting entire nations against each other, a collective awareness that the future of an entire continent is at stake—nothing seems to be missing. Yet it is all strangely unauthentic, like a literary game. Fabrice, like Don Quixote, has read too many books. His overexcited imagination attempts to impose the patterns of heroic romance on a banal and recalcitrant reality. Significantly, he considers the heterogeneous group of soldiers he has joined as "heroic" companions: "Between them and himself he saw the noble comradeship of Tasso's and Ariosto's heroes." But he forgets to tell himself that these rough hussars treat him with kindness only because he has just purchased a bottle of spirits.

Reality, vexing or ignoble, is indeed at odds with the epic dream. Thus Fabrice, who rushes gratuitously to the Emperor's defense at Waterloo, is thrown into jail as a suspected spy because of his Italian accent. Thus the grand battle reveals selfishness, cowardice, and the confusion of a humiliating rout. But it is precisely this conflict between a dream reality and the reality of actual experience that provides the interest and the comic mainspring of these pages. For Fabrice, a nineteenth-century Cherubino living out the predictions of Figaro's mocking aria "Non più andrai," is only a child who does not even know how to load a rifle. Even more naïve than Tom Jones, a model that haunted Stendhal's imagination, he shows his money to everybody, and is of course thoroughly cheated and robbed. "Tu ne sais rien de rien," is the diagnosis of the benevolent sutler who takes him under her feminine protection. The fact is that Fabrice needs more than four weeks to understand why he has been thrown into jail.

With greater zest than ever, Stendhal deflates his hero and stresses his insufficiencies. Almost with malice, he exposes him to the most trying vexations. He has him walk in rain and in mud, and at that in boots which are not his size. He has him trot on a miserable nag. Fabrice, who is so eager to see Napoleon, misses the occasion at Waterloo simply because he has had too much to drink and the Emperor gallops by too quickly. The entire episode is an exercise in incongruity and lack of synchronization. The worst indignity occurs when Fabrice, ambling proudly along on a good horse, suddenly feels himself lifted up and deposited on the road by a group of soldiers, who unceremoniously confiscate the horse. The incident is doubly ironic, since we are given to understand that the general for whom the horse is confiscated is none other than the former lieutenant Robert, the presumed father of Fabrice.

These humiliations and disheartening adventures might sober up an even greater dreamer than Fabrice. Abandoned by the soldier thieves, he sheds hot tears—from fatigue no doubt, but largely from the sorrow of finding that the world is not filled with tender and heroic comrades-in-arms who die embracing each other while reciting an *ottava rima*. Stendhal explains that his young hero is forced to undo, one by one, every dream of chivalrous friendship inspired by Tasso's *Gerusalemme liberata*. This awakening becomes altogether brutal when, a few pages later, Fabrice is wounded by soldiers who are not even enemies. The episode seems to come to a cruel conclusion as Stendhal observes with a pun:

Notre héros était ce matin-là du plus beau sang-froid du monde; la quantité de sang qu'il avait perdue l'avait délivré de toute la partie romanesque de son caractère. (5)

The absurd wound suggests a beneficent bloodletting. The Battle of Waterloo seems to function as a special therapy destined to cure Fabrice of his illusions.

Yet it would be a mistake to read these pages simply as a return to lucidity. There is an element of Candide in Fabrice, but there is also a great deal of Don Quixote. One does not recover so quickly from one's dreams. War is not, or no longer is, that generous commitment of brothers-in-arms who thirst for glory. But if the world is not what Fabrice thinks it could and should be, he is nonetheless unable to assume a prosaic view. It is not the nature but the object of his lyric and heroic quest that will change. The war chapters at the beginning of La Chartreuse simultaneously devaluate and exalt enthusiasm. Alternating between fervor and irony, Stendhal creates biting contrasts that bring out sharply the essentially "poetic" spirit of his hero. Fabrice's romantic character affirms itself the more vividly for being set against a background of parody and insignificance.

The paradoxical nature of epic parody is established most clearly in the evocation of Ariosto and Tasso, who, from the very first pages of the novel, are used as symbols of high poetry as well as pretexts for irony. It is indeed with rapture that Countess Pietranera evokes these names

as she settles near Lake Como. Her daydream is revealing:
"Among these admirably shaped hills . . . I can keep
all the illusions of Tasso's and Ariosto's descriptions. Everything is noble and tender, everything speaks of love
. . ." (2) In *Vie de Henry Brulard*, Stendhal likewise
associates Ariosto with his most cherished reveries: "I
am still moved, as I was at the age of ten when reading
Ariosto, by any tale of love, of forests (the woods and
their vast silence), of generosity." [3] And the wistful, melancholic smile of the author of *La Chartreuse* recalls the
delicately saddened smile of the poet who sang

> *Le Donne, i Cavalier, l'arme, gli amori,*
> *Le cortesie, l'audaci imprese . . .*

There can be no doubt, the lyricism of chivalry, even
though treated in an ironic mode, is not invoked in a derogatory spirit. Far from undermining the lyric illusion,
the elements of parody serve to protect it. They reveal an
oversensitive hero who is forced by the world's coarseness
to withdraw within himself. But the self-exile of an exceptional being in the face of a hostile environment also impels
him to set out in quest of that undefinable "something"
that fills the inner emptiness of the exiled individual and
that—as Camus suggests—marks the simultaneous desire
to retrace one's steps and to attend to the future.

It is in this sense that one could view the Waterloo
adventure as a preliminary stage of a spiritual itinerary.[4]
But the aim of this itinerary is bound to remain invisible
almost until the end. The frustrations and humiliations of
the war chapters are thus part of an evolution that leads
Fabrice to the discovery of essential values—values that he
may vaguely intuit but that he has to adopt in order to

understand. For he was not born with them, nor does he inherit them ready-made. Thus it is fitting that the charterhouse remain totally off-stage until the last pages of the book and that the road to this place of retirement lead through the Farnese prison tower, a prefiguration of monastic seclusion. Much like other Stendhalian heroes, Fabrice must wait until he has passed through all the successive stations of his career and must in the process relinquish many beliefs and false desires before he can discover what he was really seeking, without knowing it, from the very beginning.

To be sure, the Stendhalian paradoxes, inversions of meanings, lyrical parodies, and hidden impertinences are not made to reassure the kind of reader who wants important subjects to be treated with a tone of importance. Nothing in this respect can be more unsettling than the political motif in *La Chartreuse*. For there can be no doubt that the court of Ranuce-Ernest IV in Parma represents a serious subject. Stendhal undertook nothing less than a tableau representative of all small and large courts, in fact of the entire political climate of the reactionary, anachronistic post-Napoleonic Europe. Yet court life is presented with almost as much unreality as a comic ballet. We glimpse an operetta palace, crowded with opera buffa characters, the most lucid of whom are, moreover, perfectly aware of "playing a part." Duchess Sanseverina enjoys both the "spectacle" in which she participates and the challenges of assuming a *rôle* beside Count Mosca, who consistently views his own political activities, and politics in general, as a comical game. His official position, he complains with bitter humor, obliges him to dress up like a "personnage de comédie." (6)

In this fantasy court, ludicrous types and situations

abound. The prince lives in such terror of conspirators and revolutions that special measures have been taken: the eighty-four sentinels of his palace have been ordered to cry out a full sentence every fifteen minutes, all the doors are secured with ten locks, and at the slightest suspicious noise the minister of the Police is summoned to verify in person whether or not a Jacobin is hidden under the prince's bed. At times, the perspective is frankly that of caricature. The kicked buttocks of servile Rassi, the automatic smile of Marquise Balbi, the grotesque thinness of the prince's mistress—these farcical distortions and indignities of the human body contribute to the heavily theatrical atmosphere that reigns at Parma's court. In fact, the word "theater," as well as theatrical metaphors, occurs repeatedly. Amateur commedia dell'arte performances are the great pastime among the courtiers. But this comedy is played out at several levels. After a long "scene" with Ranuce-Ernest IV and his mother, Duchess Sanseverina observes: "I have played a comedy for one hour on the stage and for five hours in the study."

Yet this perpetual comedy stands in intimate relation to the profound themes of the book. Parody turns out to be the most suitable means for political critique of the state of affairs after 1815, precisely since much of Europe, according to Stendhal, has turned itself into a pitiful parody of the Ancien Régime. If Ranuce-Ernest attempts to imitate the gesture and the smile of a portrait of Louis XIV, if the princess is pleased to take as a model Marie de Medici, it is not merely to bring out the laughable inadequacies of given characters. What is involved in this political tragicomedy is the very spirit that transforms sunny Parma into a place of tyranny and fear. The otherwise composed Mosca, who tends to view the ebb and flow of

political power with a spectator's irony, is not devoid of a
sense of tragic indignation. "Nous sommes environnés
d'événements tragiques," he ominously confesses to
Duchess Sanseverina. (10) For he knows better than
anyone else that Parma is a city of secret threats and secret
measures. The symbolic Farnese tower, with its mysterious geometric patterns, introduces into the smiling Emi-
lian plain an almost Kafkaesque element of nightmare
and human alienation.

Mosca's statement to Duchess Sanseverina corresponds
to the author's own somber diagnosis. They share, moreover, the same ability to combine irony with passionate
indignation. In the same paragraph evoking Fabio Conti's
ludicrous terror at the mere thought of one of his prisoners escaping, Stendhal describes how these humiliated,
broken-spirited prisoners, suffering in chains in cells too
low to stand up in, pay for a *Te Deum* to celebrate their
jailor's recovery. (21) Seen in this light, the citadel becomes an allegorical figuration of human degradation
under the despotism of the modern state. Behind the fantasy tower, there is the gloomy silhouette—alas!—of the
very real Spielberg fortress where men like Silvio Pellico
and Maroncelli, some of them friends of Stendhal, were
rotting in the *carcere duro*.

Values

Political satire excludes neither pity nor the glorification of the exceptional being who accepts the rules of a wicked game but does not allow himself to be corrupted. Once again the image of Don Quixote, the eternal prototype of the glorious loser, imposes itself. Count Mosca sums up as follows one of his lessons in political realism: "At all times the vile Sancho Panças will in the long run win out over the sublime Don Quixotes." (10) The political satire, much like the epic parody, is not merely a critical weapon, but an instrument of poetry, which, through contrapuntal effects, stresses all the tender movements, all the flights of generosity, all the potential of passion—and at the same time prevents sentiment from degenerating into undisciplined sentimentality. The rhythm of *La Chartreuse* is that of the music Stendhal loved most, alternating light-hearted brio and lyrical abandon. The law of contrasts is for Stendhal a way of projecting and of protecting his most cherished dreams. In *Vie de Henry Brulard,* he explains his fondness for Ariosto: "I can be moved to tears *only after a comical passage.*" [6] A remark such as this casts light on the numerous scenes in *La Chartreuse* where comedy, pathos, and musicality echo each other. It is a most exceptional climate where laughter and sarcasm serve the exigencies of the heart.

The Stendhalian paradoxes and inversions of values, so obvious in the political motifs of *La Chartreuse,* are even more striking in the disarming immorality that reigns in the novel. This immorality is not limited to adultery and incest; it is fundamental and seems to characterize the actions and attitudes of the most lovable protagonists. Charles Maurras has called *La Chartreuse* a "charmant manuel de coquinologie politique." [7] But this *coquinologie* is by no means limited to the realm of politics. Its manifestations are extremely varied and start with the opening pages of the book. Fabrice, a most unscholarly student, receives five first prizes in his Jesuit college simply because his aunt is an important lady at the court of Prince Eugène. This aunt, in turn, accepts to marry, sight unseen, the decrepit Duke of Sanseverina-Taxis and to occupy a handsome palace and enjoy the proximity of her lover. Mosca maintains himself in power through flattery and shameless exploitation of the prince's pathological fear. As for Fabrice's choice of an ecclesiastic career, what could be more cynical than Mosca's advice and plans?

I do not claim to make of Fabrice an exemplary priest of which there are many. No, he is a nobleman first and foremost. He can remain perfectly ignorant if he so chooses. He will nonetheless become bishop and archbishop provided the prince continues to consider me useful. (6)

Mosca, one of Stendhal's most fascinating characters, is an urbane father-substitute for Fabrice. He represents the sophisticated middle-aged figure whom Stendhal, after *Le Rouge et le Noir,* liked to place side by side with his slim, adolescent heroes. The self-indulging and self-punishing tendency was to lead, in *Lamiel,* to the painful caricature of the donjuanesque hunchback, Docteur Sansfin. In *La Chartreuse,* there is no such cruel perspective; yet Mosca is made to feel the specific anguish of his age, as well as the maddening tortures of jealousy. Above all, however, he is the lucid diplomat and tender-hearted professor of cynicism. He knows that politics are a game (and who is foolish enough to object to the rules of a game?), but he also knows that absolute power justifies and sanctifies everything and that tender-heartedness is the greatest self-dupery.

It does not follow that *La Chartreuse* is a breviary of immorality. Quite the opposite. For beyond the apparent absence of conventional ethics, a special morality emerges, a morality not according to the laws and lies of society, but an authentic complex of values founded on truth and merit. Surprisingly, it is the Moscas of this world—that is, the very individuals who play at being cynical and are unable to take themselves seriously—who in their privacy forge for themselves a rigorous moral code, refuse to follow the comfortable and profitable dictates of public morality, and affirm themselves as creators of values. Mosca does not believe in the rosy, liberal formulas of political *arrivistes*. The claim to seek the happiness of the greatest number seems to him naïveté or an imposture. Mosca feels, in the first place, bound to seek the happiness of Count Mosca. But on the other hand, Stendhal explains that Mosca is "plein d'honneur," that not once has he lied to the duchess. (16)

Private and gratuitous, the morality in question rests entirely on a code of honor that freely binds human beings capable of mutual esteem. It is the morality of the Stendhalian "happy few." Its first law is not to cheat oneself. Its greatest challenge is how not to lose one's self-esteem. Stendhal's terse assessment of Duchess Sanseverina is characteristic: "She was above all a woman in perfect good faith with herself." (6) Unquestionably, it is this same ethic of honesty and severity with oneself—this same abhorrence of all poses and intellectual fraud—that plains why Fabrice, after the experience of Waterloo,

unlike so many immorally moral people who never question anything, wonders whether he has really participated
in a battle and whether he has really been brave.

It is no doubt for this creative inversion of values that
the most fervent lovers of Stendhal are fanatical "Char-
treusistes," who find in this novel the very essence of Beyliste philosophy, according to which true passion belongs
exclusively to an elite. The novel is in fact dedicated "to
the happy few"—those who, together with the author,
prize not only passion but also the modest, veiling of passion and who, though lucid, love to be the consenting victims of their illusions.

THE FREEDOM TO BECOME

Some objections might be raised. Readers insensitive to
Stendhal's mental pirouettes and to his brand of "unpoetic" poetry are likely to seek refuge in factual exegesis.
They will be tempted to explain the novel as a curious
fusion of sources, periods, and subjects, artistic perhaps
but not fully convincing—in other words, as a remarkable
potpourri. In fact, Stendhal transplanted sixteenth-cen-
tury mores into the Italy of his day; he utilized the Farnese chronicle, the memoirs of Cellini, the prison accounts of Silvio Pellico and of Andryane; he exploited
Renaissance and contemporary history, the resources of
parallels and anachronisms, his own personal experiences
(Milan, the Napoleonic army, contemporary politics),

and, of course, literary models. Among these are Rousseau, quite evidently, but also Cardinal de Retz, the bold *libertin* and enemy of Mazarin, who was master-animator of the rebellious Fronde movement, whose real name (Gondi) bears an anagrammatic resemblance to that of Dongo, and who, like Fabrice, was a younger son who also undertook an ecclesiastic career without a religious vocation, had an amorous adventure in jail, successfully escaped, and finally brought an adventurous life to an end in the solitude of a monastery.[8] This extraordinary telescoping of chronicles, memoirs, literary sources, historical facts, and private obsessions would seem to lead to a heterogeneous construction where several possible novels come to meet.

Stendhal has thus been accused of lack of focus, of dilettantism, of indulging in irritating digressions and interventions that discredit his own creation. Humorless readers have complained of elements of melodrama in *La Chartreuse,* of lack of verisimilitude, of absurd coincidences, caprices, and disguises. They have pointed out contradictions and vagueness in the themes, waverings in the conception of the characters, artificialities in the cult of energy. Even Stendhal's treatment of love, a subject of which he makes so much, has disappointed some readers, for although there are mutual attractions, at no point does the novel propose love as the adventure of a couple.

Similar exceptions, though not entirely unwarranted, indicate a lack of response to the specific vision of *La Chartreuse.* The chief difficulty for the reader not yet attuned to Stendhal is that the so-called character psychology as well as the realism of situations are here totally subordinated to the poetic perspective. For it is not a preestablished psychological reality or conceptualization that determines the poetic movement of the novel, but the poetic movement that creates its psychology and ethical substance. In other words: it is not knowledge which begets motion, but vitality, in its sheer gratuitousness, that makes possible the discovery of both the world and the self.

Love, that privileged Stendhalian subject, thus occupies the center of the novel and yet remains elusive. No determination weighs down on what for the author is essentially an élan of the spirit. Physical realities are almost entirely absent. The oppressiveness of desire, the intimacy of the lovers, the satisfaction of the senses, even tenderness persisting and transformed after shared sensual pleasures—all this Stendhal seems to eschew. The reason, however, is not prudery. The disembodiment of love accelerates the momentum of the novel. Thus there is no trace of any Romantic mysticism of the senses: no voluptuous meditations on nothingness, no exaltation of Medusan beauty, no dreams of orgies and exotic tortures. No fatal women or heavily scented temptresses strut through his books. Duchess Sanseverina is far closer to a tragic Phaedra than to a decadent Cleopatra or Salome. As for the very rare love scenes, they are either understated or of an exemplary chastity. The most detailed scene is the one that occurs in a prison cell. It occupies exactly two and a half lines:

Elle était si belle, à demi vêtue et dans cet état d'extrême passion, que Fabrice ne put résister à un mouvement preque involontaire. Aucune résistance ne fut opposée. (25)

A physical act is thus convincingly translated into a stylized gesture, and rhythm replaces description and analysis.

It is not fortuitous that the lovers embrace in a cell.

Madame de Rênal and Julien also experience their most fervent hours within the confines of prison walls. The myth of difficult and unrealizable love is altogether central to Stendhal's fiction. Hence the repeated images of bounded proximity. Hence also the touching poetry of the "glance," that almost Neoplatonic intimacy at a distance. Clélia and Fabrice delight in communicating by means of signs and secret alphabets. This cult of the obstacle and of the separation helps to explain why, toward the end of the novel, Clélia makes the strange vow to the Madonna never again to look at her lover.

In the Stendhalian mythology of love, what counts is neither intimacy nor gratification, but inner tension and the dynamics of a yearning indifferent to the present moment, already in the process of dissolution. Most important is the energy that goes into creating ideal moments. Love is for the Stendhalian heroes, at times without their fully realizing it, the chief preoccupation of their lives. They might well repeat Daphne's words in Tasso's *Aminta:*

> *Perduto è tutto il tempo*
> *Che in amar non si spende.*

But this "expenditure" of energy in the pursuit of love is worthwhile only because it commits the entire being and projects him into existence. If Stendhalian love never involves possession, this also means that the Stendhalian heroes and heroines remain free—neither possessed, nor humiliated, nor subjugated, nor betrayed. That is why Clélia's enchanting words, "Entre ici, ami de mon coeur," necessarily announce the end of the novel.

As for the Farnese dungeon where Clélia and Fabrice

love each other and which foreshadows the monastic cell
into which Fabrice will later withdraw, it symbolizes spiritual freedom and rejection of worldly cares. The prison is
thus far more than a melodramatic device. Its most meaningful aspect is suggested in the very title of the book.
In fact, references to prisons and images of claustration
crowd the pages of *La Chartreuse* from the very beginning, long before Fabrice's actual incarceration in the Farnese tower. Already in the first chapter, we are told of the
Italian patriots who are deported to Cattaro and left to die
of hunger and exposure in the subterranean caves. Soon
after, the famous imprisonment of Silvio Pellico is
evoked. Fabrice himself is jailed as soon as he reaches the
Belgian frontier. And over the entire opening section of
the novel hovers the threat as well as the lyrical prophecy
of jail.

For imprisonment is an ambiguous experience in the
world of Stendhal. It is, on the one hand, a permanent
cause for terror, as well as a concrete figuration of tyranny.
The negative references are numerous. General Pietranera is unjustly thrown into jail. (2) Fabrice is warned by
the abbé Blanès that he will end his days in a cell (4); the
threat of imprisonment hangs over him upon his return
from Waterloo (5); the Parma citadel is the "terror of all
of Lombardy," and only a "miracle" can bring prisoners
out of oblivion (6); nightmarish visions of heavy chains,
gangrened limbs, and perpetual immurement bring a "cold
sweat" to Fabrice's forehead (9, 10). "Tout vaut mieux que
le Spielberg," is his conclusion, as he conjures up horrify-
ing images of the infamous Moravian fortress where Silvio
Pellico and Maroncelli had been rotting for years. (11)
Finally, reality catches up with his fears. He is arrested,
exposed to the humiliation of handcuffs and a chain, and

subjected to the vulgar insolence of the assistant jailer, Barbone. (15)

But, on the other hand, Fabrice's very terror is mixed with a mysterious delight. It is as though Stendhal needed to exorcise the prison obsession by metamorphosing horror into poetry. A secret prison-yearning seems to propel Fabrice and to endow the notion of imprisonment with a singular prestige. Auguries and prophecies of jail seem to point to a meaningful destiny. The abbé Blanès interprets Fabrice's prison experience before Waterloo as a felicitous sign. (8) The monastic cell of Fabrice's last days is clearly prefigured in the belltower scene; so are the poetry of darkness (Blanès tells Fabrice that he must not see him again by daylight) and the notion of spiritual altitude. Blanès' tower, in part an astrological observatory, symbolically reaches toward the firmament. Fabrice, at the top of this tower, experiences the "highest sentiments" and achieves an unusual "hauteur de pensées." (9)

It is no coincidence that the church tower, for a while at least, becomes for Fabrice a protective prison; in it he experiences the characteristic Stendhalian joy of seeing without being seen. All of Stendhal's prisons are thus places of altitude and of privacy, enhanced by extensive views. That the image of happiness is subconsciously linked with the notion of claustration is made very clear by Fabrice's curious proleptic thought, upon first glimpsing Clélia: "She would make a charming prison companion." (5) The ambiguities of the terror-jail and the happiness-jail are further stressed when Clélia herself, thinking of Duchess Sanseverina's passion for Fabrice, takes pity on the prisoner's "awful solitude," and at the same time imagines his happiness in jail at knowing how much he is loved. (15)

In fact, the "positive" prison images far outnumber all
the others. The prison-wish seems stronger than the
prison-fear. When Duchess Sanseverina first visits the
Farnese tower, she is delighted by the height and by the
freshness of the air, which comes as a relief after the swel-
tering atmosphere of Parma. (6) As Fabrice climbs the
380 steps leading to the top of the prodigious tower, he can
think only of the expression of Clélia's eyes during his
arrest. (15) Clélia herself, living at the very summit of
the fortress in the midst of a prison atmosphere, enjoys
"the freedom of a convent" and the exquisite pleasures of
solitude and of an "inner life." (15) In prison, Fabrice
actually has no time to think of his unhappiness. Moreover, he undergoes a curious transformation. Imprisonment, which he feared most, now leaves him indifferent,
and he even surprises himself by "laughing in a jail." (18)
"Never have I been so happy," he confesses to himself.
(19) Now that his heart is "bound" (16), the other bonds
no longer count. And, as if to give imprisonment its fullest
symbolic meaning, the governor of the fortress has Fabrice's cell windows obstructed, allowing him only a
glimpse of the sky. The Farnese nightmare becomes part
of a vast allegory of escape.

The law of contrasts, the dynamics of contempt, and
the surprises of self-discovery are all operating here. What
Fabrice experiences in essence is a state of happy captivity, which, as Georges Blin puts it, constitutes for the
Stendhalian heroes the most efficacious "preservative"
from all noxious external influences.[9] This protection of
the self is, in fact, like a rebirth (Fabrice spends exactly
nine months in prison). Jungian critics might well be
tempted to interpret the entire tower episode as a symbol
of regeneration through the analogue of the womb. In any

case, this renewal marks a process of spiritualization. The concluding pages of the novel strongly suggest, behind their resigned and ironic sadness, an emancipation from worldly tensions. The final sentence, one of Stendhal's most ambiguous, expresses, at the same time, the detached view of the observer, the bitterness of half-truths, the immense sadness of a world now empty, and the beauty that has sought refuge elsewhere. All seems to withdraw and fade away at the end. Clélia disappears by degrees; her delicate image has the graceful *morbidezza* Stendhal loved so much in the paintings of Correggio. As for Fabrice, he quite literally undergoes a process of disincarnation. Increasingly insensitive to his immediate surroundings, yearning for a conventual retreat, he attains true beauty in his silence and in his ascetic thinness. When Clélia, after her marriage to the Marquis Crescenzi, sees Fabrice again, she is deeply moved by his extreme emaciation and by his expression, which suggests that he is now "above all that can happen in this world." (26)

The most important function of the Stendhalian prison is that it restores his heroes to their own selves—or rather, that it allows them to discover the self, and even to create it. The prison thus assumes a protective and dynamic role. It liberates one from the captivity of social existence. Julien Sorel also works out his freedom in jail; his only complaint is that the door of a prison cell cannot be locked from within. Always, this prison dream is bound up with a yearning for altitude and vast panoramas. Marcel Proust once characterized Stendhal's entire vision as a "sentiment de l'altitude se liant à la vie spirituelle."[10] One is indeed bound to recall the many "elevated" places where Stendhal's heroes discover serenity; Julien's rock, the Gothic tower in Besançon, the belltower of the abbé Blanès, the cell in the Farnese fortress. Isolation and altitude bring about the most intense moments of poetic fervor. The walls of the prison cell become the very symbol of exalted privacy.

The unity of *La Chartreuse* is obviously neither of a "documentary" nor of an "analytical" nature in the usual sense of the word. "Realism" is also a misleading term when applied to an author whose essential achievement, especially in this densely poetic novel, is of a metaphoric order. The psychology of the characters, fluid and unpredictable, is thus not an assessable reality to be demonstrated through the action, but remains subjected to the poetic vision of the whole and to the central themes of freedom in particular. For there exist hardly any a priori definitions of characters in Stendhal's novels. If Fabrice seems naïve at the beginning, if at times he seems to define himself in negative terms, it is in large measure because the author refuses to make him the prisoner of his own "essence." The void remains to be filled; and this act of filling is the very act of living. Unlike Balzac, Stendhal proposes fictional figures that are not predetermined. A hundred years before Malraux, Stendhal might have said that man is what he does, not what he hides. This emphasis on choice and action, this disregard for all the forces that may bind and determine, helps explain why Stendhal has been so dear to the Existentialist generation. His great theme, like that of the Existentialist writers, is also the theme of freedom: a freedom discovered in love, in prison, but above all through the protagonists' surprises as they watch themselves live.

Stendhal, instead of defining his characters, grants them the right to self-discovery. His ironic techniques—interventions, commentaries, disapprovals, pretended astonishment, apparent improvisations—seem to encourage them to seek themselves out on their own. It would be easy to show, for instance, that Fabrice's whole adventure is but a succession of self-revelatory glimpses. He sees himself as a volunteer, he sees himself drunk, he sees himself as a soldier who has not fought, he sees himself in a succession of roles—and each role he assumes becomes an instrument of self-understanding. A characteristic rhetoric of surprise is at work. The words "discovery" and "surprise" recur with insistence. Fabrice tells himself that he has fallen in love with Clélia, and the author explains that "he finally made this discovery." Similarly, the interrogative turn of many internal monologues suggests that the deed precedes knowledge, that action has priority over insight. "Is this a prison?"—"Is this what I feared so much?"—'Am I a hero unaware?"—"Maybe I have a noble character." (18) The ethics of freedom and of individuality—the specific Stendhalian *morale de soi à soi*—implies a pursuit of an elusive identity.

La Chartreuse de Parme is primarily a novel of quest to which all elements and motifs contribute: the thirst for experience, the voyage, the myths of the false father and of the father substitute, the apprenticeship of the world, which is in fact the hero's apprenticeship of his own possibilities, the hard lesson of a difficult and uncomfortable freedom. Time, in Stendhal's novels, is never a prisoner of necessity. To the Romantic obsession with a paralyzing self-analysis, Stendhal opposes that other Romantic obsession, the eternal becoming and the disturbing "availability" of the individual.

A disquieting note does ultimately characterize all of Stendhal's work. Faced with the self that forever eludes him, Stendhal experiences a constant uneasiness bordering on anxiety. Freedom, as Sartre has reminded us, is not an easy burden to carry. In his autobiographic texts, Stendhal insistently interrogates himself and his past in order to decipher himself—but in vain. One cannot possess oneself. The sleepless hours devoted to the questions "what am I?" and "what have I been?" yield no results. The eye needs a mirror to see itself.

But the eye of the "other," as Fabrice and all Stendhal's heroes know, has a hostile glance and is truly the enemy of our freedom. Love of freedom and fear of freedom are here complementary. And love of discovery and fear of discovery are equally interlocked. This may well be the secret of that typically Stendhalian shadow, which, like a modest veil, is cast over all precious moments and emotions. This desire to protect and yet to reveal what the author himself fails to penetrate completely is perhaps the secret tragedy behind the Stendhalian creation. Beyond the smile of Stendhal, beyond the movement and fervor of this novel, it is possible to guess the anguish of a man drawn to and at the same time distressed by the mysteries of his personality and who finds it difficult to see himself live otherwise than in the mirror of literary creation.

7

Epilogue

"She was very far from being able to judge herself and others." The heroine of *Lamiel,* the novel on which Stendhal was at work when he died, continues the line of self-questioning and self-discovering protagonists. Lamiel, the young peasant girl emancipated by books and ideas, is indeed less baffled by her lack of experience than by the unpredictability of her own character. Her interrogative turn of mind ("Am I insensitive to love?") corresponds to the need to experiment with herself as though it were possible to view one's actions and reactions with clinical detachment. Lamiel goes so far as to hire her ravisher. It is not, however, the sensation of the moment that counts; Lamiel yearns for the liberating power to see and assess. Hence her analytical bent of mind, her need to "raisonner sur tout ce qui lui était arrivé." [1]

The plot, as we know it from the written sections, notes, and sketches, suggests an even bolder character than Julien Sorel. Lamiel, a rebellious young peasant-amazon, probes all values, sees all the hypocritical flaws of society, and, like Julien, learns to use deception to protect and affirm herself. The product of a libertine education, she is free from prejudice, impatient with debility, drawn to every excess, attracted by crime, and finally becomes the mistress of a fierce outlaw. "Les crimes l'intéressaient," writes Stendhal. Early in her life, Lamiel admires the courage of energetic bandits. It is clear, however, that her fascination with crime must not be imputed to a naïve longing for sensationalism; it betrays an awareness of a disquieting inner potential. Stendhal here pushes the theme of psychological "availability" to extremes, which he would probably have found difficult to sustain. But the emphasis, in *Lamiel,* both on project and gratuitousness is surprisingly modern.

"Etonnant de modernisme," is Jacques Rivière's appraisal of *La Chartreuse* in a letter to his friend Alain-Fournier.[2] The modernity of Stendhal remains indeed striking. More singular still, this modernity has impressed succeeding generations of readers, including Taine, Bourget, Léon Blum, Charles Du Bos, Thibaudet, Gide, and, more recently, the Existentialist generation and the generation of the *nouveau roman.* There is little these minds share, or care to share, except a common attraction to Stendhal, though of course not for the same reasons. A Stendhal myth has thus come into being, which in itself deserves a nuanced study. It would provide an illuminating chapter of French intellectual history over the past hundred years. The earliest readers saw him as a master cynic. Taine and his friends at the Ecole Normale

admired the rationalist precision of this disciple of Condillac. Zola and the Naturalist school valued his lesson in
realism. The generation of Bourget and Barrès wor-
shipped him as a poet of energy. As for the tender, lyrical
Stendhal, this has been a discovery of our own times. So
is the anguish of one who ceaselessly looked into the autobiographic mirror. Yet all these generations of admirers
might agree on certain fundamental traits, which make
Stendhal more of a contemporary than either Balzac or
Hugo, even though they were almost twenty years
younger than he.

What is the secret of the freshness and proximity of
Stendhal? It is partly a matter of tone. Stendhal despises
the rhetoric of sentimentality; he is allergic to the then
fashionable amplifications, which he condemns under the
general heading of "emphase." For himself, he sought and
achieved an elegance of understatement that suggests
emotions but never pompously states them. Stendhal's
style and tone are thus simultaneously incisive and bash-
ful, ironical and yet passionate. This is the secret of Stendhal's irony: its function, contrary to first impressions, is
not so much to provoke or even to attack as it is to protect
a self-conscious sensibility. Stendhal converts the militant
irony of his masters, the eighteenth-century rationalists,
into an instrument of poetic expression. This emotional
discretion is not only effective, but corresponds to our own
ambiguous disavowal of the Romantic heritage. For we
also are averse to lyrical bombast and apologetic for our
subjectivity, while faithful in depth to what is most relevant in Romanticism. In many ways, Stendhal embodies,
ahead of his time, the inner tension and contradictions of
our own epoch.

The specific tone of Stendhal is very closely related to a

complex of moral attitudes: fear of inauthenticity, awareness of the inadequacy of language, contempt for cant,
rebellion against all forms of hypocrisy and oppression. It
represents the expression of one who has taken stock of
the incompatibilities of ethical and political realities, who
is aware that any social order implies turpitude, and who,
though resigned to the "rules of the game," is never comfortable in such a world. Stendhal's tone implies not a histrionic insurrection but a permanent state of revolt. It
affirms the priority of the individual's values and of his
privacy.

This latent anticonformity also manifests itself in the
conception of Stendhal's fictional characters, each entitled, as it were, to pursue his private dream. His heroes
are remarkably independent: ironic observers, they are
themselves ironically observed. No ties can reduce them to
the state of puppet or victim. If anything, they seem condemned to a free search for their own reality. For "reality,"
above all the reality of human psychology, remains
in Stendhalian terms subject to caution. All categories
and preestablished ideas are from the outset suspect.
When Stendhal coined the expression "génie du
soupçon"—an expression recently adopted by Nathalie
Sarraute with reference to the modern sensibility—he
meant thereby that nothing in our morally and intellectually inflationary civilization should be taken at face
value, that the danger of counterfeit lurks behind every
action and behind every statement. How to write sincere
literature under these circumstances? How to be sure that
one does not delude oneself? Long before André Gide and
today's experimental novel, Stendhal recognized the peril
of ideas. Flaubert diagnosed the lie of all clichés and false
values. But Stendhal, at the threshold of our age of ideol-

ogies, intuited the specific threat of intellectual submissiveness. Hence his early interest in the emancipatory *logique*
and his paradoxical insubordination to the very assump-
tions of a restrictive rationalism.

Stendhal's speculative approach to all experience, his
notion that reality is mobile and protean, must be assessed
in this light. His gradual attraction to the writing of fiction thus corresponds to an increasing awareness that
"truth" can be approximated only by a steady toying with
possibilities, by projecting into poetic hypotheses the un-
assimilated, and perhaps unassimilable, data of personal
experience. From autobiography to fiction: the relationship is not merely that of a genetic nature; it suggests the
effort to transcend the limitations and falsifications of intellectual smugness. For impersonation leads to self-identification, and the purpose of Stendhal's disguises is not to
hide but to discover. The mask is not there to elude but
to reveal.

Such a perspective stresses with particular intensity the
clash between collective and private values, which remain largely irreconcilable. No evaluation of Stendhal
can afford to neglect the historical and sociological context. It is not fortuitous that he bridges two periods, and
that his formative years coincide with that moment in history when the exigencies of the state and the demands of
human rights become equally clamorous and uncompro-
mising. Perhaps the single most modern aspect of Stendhal's work is precisely this clear consciousness of the crisis and contradictions of modern humanism that subject
the individual to a collective despotism and render political freedom illusory. To believe that liberty can be
achieved by political revolution is perhaps the worst delu-
sion, according to Stendhal. What matters in a world in-

creasingly hostile to a nonconformist stance is to salvage
the prerogatives of personal expression, to salvage the
very notion of the individual. But such a survival can be
achieved and be meaningful only if all external imperatives, especially those intended to serve political expedi-
ency, are constantly challenged and subverted. What is
involved is not anarchism but self-protection. Stendhal is
probably the first European writer to intuit that intellect
had become both a cause for alienation and an instrument
of heroic critique. Irving Howe is no doubt right: Stendhal speaks for an increasingly "homeless" intelligentsia.[3]
But it is, one should add, a poetic estrangement. Julien
Sorel's prison destiny has more than one thing in common
with that of Camus' *étranger*: society condemns them for
not playing its game; yet in their refusal, both have found
dignity and moral salvation, despite their faults.

The prison image is indeed central to Stendhal's work.
It represents an indictment of society, as well as a poetic
figuration of man's inner freedom. It also constitutes the
metaphoric point of contact between psychological and
political levels of meaning. The interdependence of these
political and psychological orders, transmuted into dramatic and poetic terms, is the measure of Stendhal's realism, which is not to be confused with the attempt to re-
produce the lines and surfaces of a physical world or the
accurate inventory of documented facts. Stendhal interprets and translates. But this translation is also responsible
for his more subtle rendering of the interaction of individual and society than is to be found in the work of any
other French novelist of his time.

Stendhal's response to the tensions he perceives is never
simplistic. On the one hand, he sees history as the great
modern tragedy, as a new form of oppression, collective

and anonymous. Born a few years before the collapse of
the Ancien Régime, he was a child during the great political upheavals, an adolescent during the Consulate, an
official during the Empire, a writer and dilettante under
the Restoration, a consul under the July Monarchy. His
entire existence, one might say, was placed under the
signs of revolution, time, and change. Few writers were as
conscious as he of the acceleration of history. Few sensed
as keenly as he that lip service to the tyrant in power had
become the first condition for successful rebellion. For the
new forms of tyranny could no longer be frontally opposed. They were too amorphous, too occult. A new form
of courage had become necessary, the courage to momen-
tarily betray one's secret beliefs in order to better safe-
guard them. Even in childhood, Stendhal understood that
deception was the weapon of slaves. He would certainly
have subscribed to the opinion of the philosopher Brice
Parain that intellectuals, in our world of oppressive
régimes and societies, are those who know best how to say
"yes," while meaning "no."

But on the other hand, Stendhal is not satisfied with
mental sabotage. The pursuit of freedom is not merely a
defensive undertaking, exposing the vices and the cruelty
of oppression. Stendhal's novels imply a positive commitment to an ethical quest. Or rather, they propose the fictional account of a "moral" enterprise. Stendhal's ethics of
freedom cannot be reduced to an adventure in nonconformity. The Beyliste obsession with self-esteem is not a
simple manifestation of narcissism. It is part of that poetry
of integrity which, in almost every case, engages the Stendhalian heroes on the road toward a surrender of worldly
ambitions.

Even in his nonfictional writings, the underlying structures of Stendhal's themes of freedom remain those of a novelist. This is no doubt what lends them their nuanced meanings as well as their poetic resonance. Stendhal's work fuses, in a unique manner, the moral perspective of the Idéologue with the fictional vision of the Egotist. This is why any attempt to read his novels as mere illustrations of his theories is bound to betray both his art and his intellectual attitudes. It is true that his writings remain personal, and to some readers irritatingly subjective. It is also true that Stendhal is not a creator of a fictional "world" in the sense that Balzac, Dickens, and Proust are. But although he was driven by an essentially autobiographic urge, it can be said that the autobiographic optics are precisely those that, in his case, allow for a creative separation from the self. The diarist and the memorialist precede the novelist and are absorbed by him. For fiction not only makes it possible to interpret experience, it poses, in dramatic terms, the preoccupying relationship between necessity and freedom.

The techniques and patterns of the novel, as handled by Stendhal, are indeed well suited to conveying his central thematic concerns. Paul Valéry, in a somewhat hasty essay, blames Stendhal for his inveterate clowning, for consistently robbing his characters of the spotlight in order to make of his novel the private theater of his consciousness.[4] What Valéry, with his general prejudice against the novel, fails to understand is that Stendhal's perpetual "presence," his playacting at being surprised by his own creation, as well as the priority of the writing process over the dictates of a plot, while freeing him from the restrictions of an artificial impersonality, also grant his characters the very autonomy and unpredictability that are so essential to the development of his most serious motifs.

The same is true of the temporal and affective patterns of Stendhal's novels. It is not by chance that all of his fictional works present very young heroes, adolescents even, whose characters remain to be shaped. Time has not yet imposed a fixed mask, nor has it eroded their will to become. Moreover, time appears ultimately reversible: memory liberates the autobiographer as well as the fictional heroes from the determinism of an implacable temporal order, by offering them the possibilities of an invention *à rebours*. The prison cell thus represents escape, for it is there that affective and involuntary memory provides, in almost Proustian terms, a challenge to contingency.

Passion itself loses, with Stendhal, all vestiges of its passive sense. A projection rather than a submission, an unrealizable desire rather than a corruptible reality, love also marks a transcending of time. Neither is it by coincidence that the greatest ecstasies of love take place behind austere and quasi-monastic prison walls. Ultimately, it is a freedom from all worldly ambitions, an almost spiritual elation, that Julien Sorel and Fabrice del Dongo achieve.

This freedom, which the proximity of death accentuates, is, however, not without sadness. The central prison metaphor, which raises Stendhal's two major novels to the level of high romance, invites dreams of liberation; but it also suggests that freedom remains a prisoner's dream, and that man's true vocation is solitude.

Notes *

CHAPTER 1

1. *Mélanges intimes et marginalia* (Paris: Le Divan, 1936), II, 277.
2. Jean Starobinski, "Stendhal pseudonyme," in *L'Oeil vivant* (Paris: Gallimard, 1961), pp. 193–196.
3. *Correspondance* (Paris: Le Divan, 1934), IX, 310. For Rousseau's influence on Stendhal, see Victor Brombert, "Stendhal, lecteur de Rousseau," *Revue des Sciences Humaines*, 92 (October–December 1958), 463–482.
4. See Jean-Paul Sartre, *L'Etre et le Néant* (Paris: Gallimard, 1943), pp. 153–193, 536–585; and *Baudelaire* (Paris: Gallimard, 1947), pp. 180–223.
5. Gilbert Durand, *Le Décor mythique de la Chartreuse de Parme* (Paris: José Corti, 1961), p. 126.
6. *Ibid.*
7. Georges Blin, *Stendhal et les problèmes du roman* (Paris: José Corti, 1954), pp. 115–176.

CHAPTER 2

1. *Mélanges de Littérature* (Paris: Le Divan, 1933), III, 417.
2. *Pensées. Filosofia Nova* (Paris: Le Divan, 1931), I, 22, 92, 120, 123, 153, 170, 226, 237, 245, 246–247, 250; II, 58–59, 64, 66, 118, 179–180, 200.

---

* Works by Stendhal are listed by title only. For a complete list of his works see p. 197.

3. Jean Prévost, *La Création chez Stendhal* (Paris: Mercure de France, 1951), pp. 93–103.

4. *Journal* (Paris: Le Divan, 1937), IV, 171.

5. *Courrier anglais*, Henri Martineau (ed.) (Paris: Le Divan, 1935–1936), I, 184–185; IV, 88–89.

6. *Ibid.*, II, 269; III, 173, 441.

7. An interesting study by Peter Brooks, *The Novel of Wordliness*, will be published by the Princeton University Press, Spring 1969.

8. *Mélanges intimes et marginalia* (Paris: Le Divan, 1936), I, 67.

9. *Histoire de la peinture en Italie* (Paris: Le Divan, 1929), I, 24–33, 168.

10. *Rome, Naples et Florence en 1817* (Paris: Le Divan, 1956), p. 46.

11. *Mélanges de Littérature*, I, 5–27.

12. There was supposedly, in the seventeenth century, one Babilano Pallavicino who suffered from the infirmity that later went by his name.

13. *Mélanges intimes et marginalia*, II, 71.

14. See F. W. J. Hemmings, *Stendhal: A Study of His Novels* (Oxford: The Clarendon Press, 1964), p. 63. Hemmings suggests that the basic plot of *Armance* is almost identical with that of Stendhal's incompleted play *Les Deux Hommes* (1803–1804), which Stendhal intended to be something of an "obstacle course."

15. Georges Blin, "Etude sur 'Armance,' " Introduction to *Armance* (Paris: Edition de la Revue Fontaine, 1946), pp. lx–lxxviii.

16. For a more substantial discussion of ironic intervention in *Armance*, see Victor Brombert, *Stendhal et la voie oblique* (Paris: Presses Universitaires de France, 1954), pp. 6–10.

CHAPTER 3

1. Prosper Mérimée, *Lettres à Stendhal* (Paris: Le Divan, 1947), I, 221; Balzac, *Oeuvres Diverses* (Paris: Conard,

1938), II, 114–115; T. S. Eliot, "Beyle or Balzac," *Athenaeum*, 4648 (May 30, 1919), 393.

2. For a more elaborate discussion of this passage, see the analysis of the French text in Victor Brombert, *Stendhal et la voie oblique* (Paris: Presses Universitaires de France, 1954), pp. 20–21.

3. Jean-Pierre Richard, "Connaissance et tendresse chez Stendhal," in *Littérature et Sensation* (Paris: Editions du Seuil, 1954), pp. 17–116.

4. *Pensées. Filosofia Nova* (Paris: Le Divan, 1931), I, 153.

5. See the Appendix to *Le Rouge et le Noir* (Paris: Garnier, 1939), pp. 514, 525.

6. *Vie de Henry Brulard* (Paris: Le Divan, 1949), I, 203. On the amazon motif, see Gilbert Durand, *Le Décor mythique de la Chartreuse de Parme* (Paris: José Corti, 1961), pp. 112–125.

7. See the Appendix to *Le Rouge et le Noir*, pp. 515, 521.

8. For some enlightening comments on this subject, see Louis Aragon, *La Lumière de Stendhal* (Paris: Denoël, 1954), pp. 66–78.

9. *Vie de Henry Brulard*, I, 473–474.

CHAPTER 4

1. See *Lucien Leuwen*, Henry Debraye (ed.) (Paris: Champion, 1927), II, 418, 441. See also *Mélanges intimes et marginalia* (Paris: Le Divan, 1936), II, 281.

2. *Lucien Leuwen*, Henry Debraye (ed.), see footnote 1; Henri Rambaud (ed.) (Paris: Bossard, 1929); *Mélanges intimes et marginalia*, Henri Martineau (ed.) (Paris: Le Divan, 1936), II, 206–287.

3. *Correspondance* (Paris: Le Divan, 1934), X, 268. *Mélanges intimes et marginalia*, II, 254.

4. *Mélanges intimes et marginalia*, II, 211, 215, 271. Italics my own.

5. Jean Prévost, *La Création chez Stendhal* (Paris: Mercure de France, 1951), p. 311.

6. *Mélanges intimes et marginalia*, II, 254.

7. *Ibid.*, II, 262.
8. *Ibid.*, II, 216–217, 281, 282.
9. *Ibid.*, II, 268, 277.
10. *Correspondance*, X, 268.
11. *Mélanges intimes et marginalia*, II, 212, 248, 261, 276.
12. *Ibid.*, II, 217, 260.
13. *Ibid.*, II, 237, 258.
14. *Correspondance*, X, 272.
15. Gilbert Durand, "Lucien Leuwen ou l'héroïsme à l'envers," *Stendhal Club*, I, 3 (April 1959), 201–225.

CHAPTER 5

1. *Histoire de la peinture en Italie* (Paris: Le Divan, 1929), II, 64–67.
2. *Napoléon* (Paris: Le Divan, 1933), II, 172–190.
3. *Racine et Shakespeare* (Paris: Le Divan, 1928), pp. 45, 198, 200.
4. Quoted by Henri Martineau in his introduction to *Rome, Naples et Florence en 1817* (Paris: Le Divan, 1954), p. xix.
5. *Vie de Henry Brulard* (Paris: Le Divan, 1949), p. 483.
6. *Histoire de la peinture en Italie*, I, 205; II, 35, 36, 191–192; *Rome, Naples et Florence* (Paris: Champion, 1919), I, 90.
7. *Rome, Naples et Florence en 1817* (Paris: Le Divan, 1956), p. 167.
8. Luigi Foscolo Benedetto, *La Parma di Stendhal* (Florence: Sansoni, 1950), p. 25–44.
9. *Chroniques italiennes* (Paris: Le Divan, 1929), I, 6.
10. *Promenades dans Rome* (Paris: Le Divan, 1931), II, 327; *Mélanges intimes et marginalia* (Paris: Le Divan, 1936), II, 184, 187.
11. See Appendix III to *La Chartreuse de Parme* (Paris: Garnier, 1942).
12. *Chroniques italiennes* (Paris: Le Divan, 1929), II, 259. These remarks on Stendhal's aversion to violence were originally developed in my essay, "Stendhal, Analyst or

Amorist?" *Yale French Studies*, 11 (Summer 1953), 39–48.

13. *Chroniques italiennes*, II, 61.

14. *Ibid.*, I, 13.

15. *Ibid.*, I, 29, 36.

16. *Ibid.*, I, 86, 101–102.

CHAPTER 6

1. Some of the ideas developed in this chapter were originally sketched out in my introduction to *Stendhal: A Collection of Critical Essays* (Englewood Cliffs, N.J.: Prentice-Hall, 1962) and were the basis of a paper read at the "Congrès Stendhalien" held in Parma in May 1967.

2. Enrico Panzacchi, "De Stendhal," *Nuova Antologia* (December 1, 1885), XXIII, 377–395.

3. *Vie de Henry Brulard* (Paris: Le Divan, 1949), I, 233.

4. For a view of *Le Rouge et le Noir* and *La Chartreuse de Parme* as fictional accounts of spiritual pilgrimages, see Claude-Edmonde Magny, *Histoire du Roman français depuis 1918* (Paris: Éditions du Seuil, 1950), I, 338.

5. For a discussion of the theatrical images in relation to the realism of *La Chartreuse*, see Judd D. Hubert, "The Devaluation of Reality in the *Chartreuse de Parme*," in Victor Brombert, *Stendhal: A Collection of Critical Essays*, pp. 95–100.

6. *Vie de Henry Brulard*, I, 445.

7. On Stendhal as "docteur d'une nouvelle immoralité," see Charles Maurras, Preface to *Rome, Naples et Florence en 1817* (Paris: Champion, 1919), I, 34.

8. For echoes of Rousseau in Stendhal's writings, see Victor Brombert, "Stendhal, lecteur de Rousseau," *Revue des Sciences Humaines*, 92 (October–December 1958), 463–482. For a discussion of Cardinal de Retz as a possible source for *La Chartreuse*, see Luigi Magnani, "L'Idea della Chartreuse," *Paragone*, 38 (February 1953), 5–27.

9. Georges Blin, *Stendhal et les problèmes du roman* (Paris: José Corti, 1954), p. 107. Since writing this book, I have

read with great pleasure Stephen Gilman's *The Tower as Emblem* (Frankfurt: Vittorio Klostermann, 1967), which reaches similar conclusions about Fabrice's freedom in captivity.

10. Marcel Proust, *A la Recherche du temps perdu* (Paris: Bibliothèque de la Pléiade, 1954), III, 377.

CHAPTER 7

1. *Lamiel* (Paris: Le Divan, 1948), pp. 84, 223, 246, 252.
2. Jacques Rivière and Alain-Fournier, *Correspondance, 1905–1906* (Paris: Gallimard, 1926), I, 197.
3. Irving Howe develops his ideas on Stendhal as a political novelist in "Stendhal: The Politics of Survival," in *Politics and the Novel* (New York: Horizon Press, 1957), pp. 25–50.
4. Paul Valéry, "Stendhal," in *Variété II* (Paris: Gallimard, 1930), pp. 88–89.

Chronology

1783 Birth of Henri Beyle (Stendhal) in Grenoble.
1790 Death of Stendhal's mother.
1796–1799 Studies at the Ecole Centrale in Grenoble. His passion for mathematics.
1799 Departure for Paris to enter the Ecole Polytechnique.
1800–1802 Protected by his relative Pierre Daru, he obtains a commission in the army and leaves for Italy. First impressions of Milan and La Scala. Translates Goldoni, begins to keep a regular diary (*Journal*) and contemplates a literary career.
1802–1806 Formative years in Paris. Reads the Idéologues (Helvétius, Cabanis, Destutt de Tracy), studies acting, works unsuccessfully on plays. Falls in love with an actress and, in 1805, follows her to Marseille.
1806–1814 Pierre Daru, now chief of the army commissary, obtains for him an important administrative position in the army. Stationed in Germany, becomes Auditeur au Conseil d'Etat and spends some time in Paris, leading the life of a dandy. Important trip to Italy in 1811, where Angela Pietragrua becomes his mistress. Decides to write a history of Italian painting. Participates in the retreat from Moscow in 1812, is Intendant in Sagan. In 1814, helps organize the military defense of the Dauphiné.

1814–1821 Self-exile to Milan, where he lives as a dilettante. Frequents groups of Italian Liberals, enjoys Italian art and music. Interested in political and literary polemics. Begins early version of *Vie de Napoléon*. Unrequited love for Métilde Dembowski. Unhappy, and politically suspect, returns to Paris in 1821.

1815 *Vies de Haydn, de Mozart et de Métastase.*

1817 *Histoire de la peinture en Italie.*
Rome, Naples et Florence en 1817 (uses the famous pseudonym Stendhal for the first time).

1821–1830 Settles in Paris as a man of letters. Reputation as a wit. Financial stress. Trips to England and contributions to English publications. Polemics about Romanticism. Several important love affairs: Clémentine Curial, Alberthe de Rubempré, Giulia Martini. Intense literary production, culminating in *Le Rouge et le Noir*.

1822 *De l'Amour.*

1823 *Racine et Shakespeare,* Part I.
Vie de Rossini.

1825 *Racine et Shakespeare,* Part II.

1827 *Armance* (first novel).

1829 *Promenades dans Rome.*

1830 *Le Rouge et le Noir.*

1831–1836 After a brief stay in Trieste, is appointed consul in the Papal town of Civitavecchia. Loneliness, illness, boredom, long absences in Rome. Writes his autobiographical *Souvenirs d'égotisme* and *Vie de Henry Brulard,* as well as the unfinished novel *Lucien Leuwen* (all of them published after his death). Discovers manuscripts of Italian Renaissance chronicles.

1836–1839 Prolonged leave in Paris, thanks to the protection of Count Molé. Begins *Mémoires sur Napoléon.* An intensely productive period.

1837–1839 *Chroniques italiennes.*

1838 *Mémoires d'un touriste.*

1839 *La Chartreuse de Parme*. Begins *Lamiel* (unfinished novel). Return to Civitavecchia.
1841 Back in Paris, on health leave, after an attack.
1842 Dies in Paris, after an apoplectic stroke.

Works by Stendhal

The most complete edition of Stendhal's works was edited by Henri Martineau (Paris: Le Divan, 1927–1937), 79 volumes. I have made use of this edition, except for the following works, which appear in the more recent editions listed below:

> *La Chartreuse de Parme.* Henri Martineau (ed.). Paris: Garnier, 1942.
>
> *De l'Amour.* Henri Martineau (ed.). Paris: Le Divan, 1957.
>
> *Rome, Naples et Florence en 1817.* Henri Martineau (ed.). Paris: Le Divan, 1956.
>
> *Le Rouge et le Noir.* Henri Martineau (ed.). Paris: Garnier, 1939.
>
> *Souvenirs d'égotisme.* Henri Martineau (ed.). Paris: Le Divan, 1950.
>
> *Vie de Henry Brulard.* Henri Martineau (ed.). Paris: Le Divan, 1949.

There also exists a convenient Pléiade edition, edited by Henry Martineau (Paris: Bibliothèque de la Pléiade, 1959–1961), 3 volumes, containing the novels, the short stories, and the autobiographic writings.

Victor del Litto is presently preparing a complete *Correspondance* of Stendhal (Paris: Bibliothèque de la Pléiade). Two volumes have already appeared (1962, 1967).

I have, in all cases, based my analyses on the French texts. All translations appearing in my book are my own.

Recently published or reissued English translations include the following:

The Abbess of Castro, and other Tales. C. K. Scott Moncrieff (tr.). New York: Boni and Liveright, 1926.

Armance. C. K. Scott Moncrieff (tr.). New York: Boni and Liveright, 1928.

Armance. Gilbert and Suzanne Sale (tr.). Chester Springs, Pa.: Dufour Editions, 1960.

The Charterhouse of Parma. C. K. Scott Moncrieff (tr.). New York: Modern Library, 1925 (Also in Signet paperback).

Féder; or, The Moneyed Husband. H. R. L. Edwards (tr.). Philadelphia: Dufour Editions, 1962.

Lamiel. T. W. Earp (tr.). New York: New Directions, 1952.

The Life of Henri Brulard. Catherine Alison Phillips (tr.). New York: Knopf, 1925.

Life of Rossini. Richard N. Coe (tr.). New York: Criterion Books, 1957.

Lucien Leuwen. Louise Varèse (tr.). New York: New Directions, 1950. 2 vols.

Memoirs of a Tourist. Allan Seager (tr.). Evanston, Ill.: Northwestern University Press, 1962.

Memoirs of Egotism. Hannah and Matthew Josephson (tr.). New York: Lear, 1949.

On Love. H. B. V. (tr.). New York: Boni and Liveright, 1927 (Also in Universal Library, Grosset paperback).

The Private Diaries of Stendhal. Robert Sage (tr.). Garden City, New York: Doubleday, 1954 (Also in Norton paperback).

The Red and the Black. C. K. Scott Moncrieff (tr.). New York: Modern Library, 1953 (Also in Bantam paperback, tr. Bair).

A Roman Journal. Haakon Chevalier (tr.). New York: Orion Press, 1957 (Also in Crowell Collier paperback).

Rome, Naples, and Florence. Richard N. Coe (tr.). New York: G. Braziller, 1960.

Scarlet and Black. Margaret R. B. Shaw (tr.). New York: Penguin Books, 1965.

Selected Journalism from the English Reviews. Edited with Introduction by Geoffrey Strickland. New York: Grove Press, 1959.

The Shorter Novels of Stendhal. C. K. Scott Moncrieff (tr.). New York: Liveright, 1946.

Selected Reading

The books listed below, most of which were published during the past twenty years, offer a variety of perspectives on modern Stendhal criticism.

Adams, Robert M. *Stendhal: Notes on a Novelist.* New York: Noonday Press, 1959. An incisive, intelligent study bridging literary criticism and biography.

Aragon, Louis. *La Lumière de Stendhal.* Paris: Denoël, 1954. Contains some provocative discussions of Stendhal's realism.

Arbelet, Paul. *La Jeunesse de Stendhal.* Paris: Champion, 1919. A detailed biography of Stendhal's early years.

Atherton, John. *Stendhal.* London: Bowes and Bowes, 1965. An incisive, short general study.

Auerbach, Erich. "In the Hôtel de La Mole," in *Mimesis.* Princeton, N.J.: Princeton University Press, 1953. A masterful analysis based on a scene in *Le Rouge et le Noir.*

Bardèche, Maurice. *Stendhal romancier.* Paris: Editions de la Table Ronde, 1947. An intelligent discussion of Stendhal's thought and craft, colored, however, by a rightist political perspective.

Blin, Georges. *Stendhal et les problèmes du roman* and *Stendhal et les problèmes de la personnalité.* Paris: José Corti, 1954 and 1958. Fundamental and highly complex studies of the patterns of Stendhal's mind and art.

Blum, Léon. *Stendhal et le beylisme.* Paris: Albin Michel, 1930. A general study containing many nuanced remarks on Stendhal's life and on his typical heroes.

Brombert, Victor. *Stendhal et la voie oblique.* Paris: Presses

Universitaires de France, 1954. A study of Stendhal's irony and sensibility as revealed through his intrusions in the novels.

—————— (ed.). *Stendhal: A Collection of Critical Essays.* Englewood Cliffs, N.J.: Prentice-Hall, 1962. A collection of modern Stendhal criticism containing studies by Martin Turnell, Erich Auerbach, Jean Prévost, Raymond Giraud, Irving Howe, Judd D. Hubert, Léon Blum, Jean Starobinski, Jean-Pierre Richard, Simone de Beauvoir, and Victor Brombert.

Del Litto, Victor. *La Vie intellectuelle de Stendhal.* Paris: Presses Universitaires de France, 1959. Studies the genesis and evolution of Stendhal's ideas during his formative years.

Durand, Gilbert. *Le Décor mythique de la Chartreuse de Parme.* Paris: José Corti, 1961. A very suggestive discussion of the novel in archetypal and mythic terms.

Dutourd, Jean. *The Man of Sensibility.* New York: Simon and Schuster, 1961. An amusing and quite "Stendhalian" meditation on Stendhal and related subjects.

Gilman, Stephen. *The Tower as Emblem.* Frankfurt: Vittorio Klostermann, 1967. An inspired, thematic study of Chapters 8, 9, 19, and 20 of *La Chartreuse de Parme,* focusing on the symbolism of the Farnese tower.

Giraud, Raymond. "Stendhal—the Bridge and the Gap Between Two Centuries," in *The Unheroic Hero.* New Brunswick, N.J.: Rutgers University Press, 1957. Studies the attitudes of Stendhal and of Lucien Leuwen in the light of nineteenth-century "bourgeois" values.

Hemmings, F. W. J. *Stendhal, A Study of His Novels.* Oxford: The Clarendon Press, 1964. A perceptive discussion of Stendhal's heroes and of the themes of his novels.

Imbert, H. F. *Les Métamorphoses de la liberté.* Paris: José Corti, 1967. A well-documented study of Stendhal's attitudes toward the Restoration and the Risorgimento.

Levin, Harry. *The Gates of Horn: A Study of Five French Realists.* New York: Oxford University Press, 1963. Contains an important chapter on Stendhal.

Martineau, Henri. *Le Coeur de Stendhal.* 2 vols. Paris: Albin

Michel, 1952, 1953. A most authoritative and very read-able biography.

Prévost, Jean. *La Création chez Stendhal*. Paris: Mercure de France, 1951. A very perceptive study of Stendhal's writings, stressing problems of style and literary technique.

Richard, Jean-Pierre. "Connaissance et tendresse chez Stendhal," in *Littérature et sensation*. Paris: Editions du Seuil, 1954. Studies in depth the basic patterns of Stendhal's imagination, with emphasis on his sensory perceptions.

Starobinski, Jean. "Stendhal pseudonyme," in *L'Oeil vivant*. Paris: Gallimard, 1961. A brilliant discussion of Stendhal's need for masks and intellectual disguises.

Turnell, Martin. *The Novel in France*. New York: New Directions, 1951. Contains a valuable chapter on Stendhal.

Index